Sit 'n Go S

Expert Advice fo ...ng
One-Table Poker Tournaments

By

Collin Moshman

A product of Two Plus Two Publishing
www.twoplustwo.com

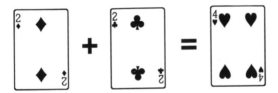

FIRST EDITION
FIRST PRINTING: APRIL 2007

Printing and Binding
Creel Printing Co.
Las Vegas, Nevada

Printed in the United States of America

Sit 'n Go Strategy
Expert Advice for Beating
One-Table Poker Tournaments

Copyright © 2007 by
Two Plus Two Publishing LLC

For information contact:

Two Plus Two Publishing LLC
32 Commerce Center Drive
Suite H-89
Henderson, NV 89014
www.twoplustwo.com

ISBN: 1-880685-39-6
ISBN13: 978-1-880685-39-6

Dedication

To the Glorious Sit 'n Go:

You have treated me well with riches,
May you now do the same for my readers.

Table of Contents

i

About Collin Moshman

Collin Moshman graduated in 2003 with an honors degree in theoretical math from Caltech. Later that year, he began playing $0.10-$0.25 cash no-limit hold 'em and $6 sit 'n go's. By the time he was crushing the $215's sit 'n go's and beyond, he abandoned his post-graduate studies in economics to focus on sit 'n go poker as a full-time career.

During a term of study at Cambridge University, Collin visited Scotland with his father to hoist the famed *clach cuid fir* — the Scottish stones of manhood. His exploits are detailed in "An Up-Lifting Journey," appearing in the June 2003 issue of MILO Strength Journal. Other interests of Collin include racquetball, dealer's choice home poker games, free-market economics, and 19th century music.

Lastly, Collin has the Stu Ungar-like quality of wanting to bet on just about everything. His current wager is that he can teach his arts-oriented girlfriend, Katie, to play poker better than she can teach him to sing. Collin considers this bet a lock, barring sudden possession by Frank Sinatra.

Acknowledgments

Thanks foremost to Mason, David, and Two Plus Two Publishing LLC for their invaluable strategic and editorial advice. Thank you also to all the early poker pioneers, software entrepreneurs, forum posters, and all others who have contributed to make the sit 'n go the vibrant and lucrative game it is today.

I would like to thank my Mom and Dad, Tamara and Marc. I would also like to thank all my friends and family, especially Dan and Ed, for their support. A special thanks goes to my brother Jesse, who taught me over countless head's up no-limit sessions that the aggressive player takes the cash.

And a heartfelt thank you to Katie, who supported and encouraged this project from the beginning. And finally a very special thanks to James Arnote who designed the cover through a cover design contest on www.twoplustwo.com. It looks great.

Introduction

The sit-n-go (SNG) is a one-table 9 or 10-player tournament with prizes for first, second, and third places.

Sit 'n go's do not pay for high chip counts or early leads. The only thing that matters in determining payout is how many people have already been eliminated once you are through playing. With 10 players, for instance:

- If 0-6 players have been eliminated and you bust out, you win nothing.

- If 7 players have been eliminated and you bust out, you win 20 percent of the prize pool.

- If 8 players have been eliminated and you bust out, you win 30 percent of the prize pool.

- If you are the last player remaining, you win 50 percent of the prize pool.

The strategy we put forth is to play a cautious game when the blinds are small and any pot you play puts you at risk for early elimination, yet aggressively when the blinds are large and you begin your quest to accumulate all the chips in play. This is a relatively simple, yet brutally effective approach.

In particular, you should:

1. When the blinds are low, play only hands you recognize as being profitable, and avoid big pots unless you are confident in your winning chances.

2. When the blinds are moderate, begin blind-stealing or re-stealing with decent hands in late position.

3. When the blinds are high, raise big to win them often. If necessary, make these raises with marginal hands that would normally be avoided.

Each of the first three parts of this book will give the details of low-blind, mid-blind, and high-blind play. The remaining sections deals with important topics for serious sit 'n go players such as multi-tabling, software, and table selection. But first, I need to address the following note:

> **Note:** Throughout this book to make the writing simpler, I'll refer to "$X in tournament chips" as just "tX." However, when I say "$X" it will be referring to actual money. In any case, the context should make it clear to which case is appropriate.

The default blind structure used in the examples is a fast 10-handed structure with a starting chip stack of t2,000.

Level 1: t20-t40	Level 6: t300-t600
Level 2: t30-t60	Level 7: t400-t800
Level 3: t50-t100	Level 8: t600-t1,200
Level 4: t100-t200	Level 9: t1,000-t2,000
Level 5: t200-t400	

The concepts apply equally to any similar online structure such as 9-handed or starting stacks and blinds of t1,000 and t5-t10, respectively. Aspects of play that vary heavily with buy-in are noted explicitly throughout this book.

Part One

Low-Blind Play

Low-Blind Play

Introduction

Suppose you buy in for a 10-handed $215 SNG, and thus exchange $200 — after the house take — for $2,000 (in tournament chips). The worth of each chip, then, appears to be 10 cents:

$$\$0.10 = \frac{\$200 \text{ buy - in}}{\$2,000 \text{ in chips}}$$

And yet, if you win the tournament, your prize for collecting all $20,000 in chips is $1,000, not $2,000, implying a cash-out value of only 5 cents per chip:

$$\$0.05 = \frac{\$1,000 \text{ buy - in}}{\$20,000 \text{ in chips}}$$

The difference in chip value is because those who place third and second win money, despite having no chips to cash out at elimination. If the tournament were winner-take-all instead, each chip would be identically worth 10 cents.

> But in a standard 3-payout sit 'n go structure, chips decline in value. The more chips you have, the less each chip is worth. Similarly, the fewer chips you have, the more each individual chip is worth.[1]

Again, this is because you can win back at most 4 to 5 buyins in dollars, even if you increase your chip count to a near-maximal 8 or 9 times the original stack size.

This chip distinction is very different from cash play where all red or blue chips have the same worth. In cash play, assessing how much money you expect to make from a play is the same as determining how many chips you expect to earn on average. But in a sit 'n go, where chips have different values, winning chips is not the same as winning money.

And since it is only money that we are concerned with, we begin with the first of our "Critical Poker Concepts."

---

[1] This aspect of tournaments was first pointed out by Mason Malmuth in his book *Gambling Theory and Other Topics*.

Critical Poker Concepts

Tournament Equity

Tournament equity is your "rightful share" of a tournament. Suppose the sit 'n go you just began was somehow repeated over and over, with nothing changing — the players, their positions, mental states, distractions — except the ever-varying cards. Take the amount you win/lose on average, and this is your equity.

So suppose you are playing a 10-handed $11 sit 'n go (with a $10 buy-in and $1 rake). Ten players contribute exactly $10 to the prize pool, so adding each player's equity will always come to $100. A reasonable first guess, then, is that going into the sit 'n go, each player has $10 in equity, with the house getting its guaranteed $10. But since all players will have different skills (most importantly), but also relative positions, responses to other players in the sit 'n go, etc., individual equities may vary considerably.

In a given $11 sit 'n go, the actual equity might break down as follows:

Player	Comments	Equity
The Novice	First sit 'n go ever, no poker experience	$5
The Recklessly Aggressive	Wants to take all the chips or go broke quickly	$8
The Calling Station	Hits the "Call" button every hand until he hits the nuts or someone plays back	$7

The Loose and Predictable Player	Has tight player to immediate left, though	$10
The Very Loose	But has good instincts	$10
The Tight-Aggressive	On tilt from several recent drawouts	$11
The Tight-Passive	Tight, very timid player.	$11
The Loose-Aggressive	Plays many hands, betting and raising rather than calling	$11
The Tight-Aggressive	Playing 6 tables at one time	$12
The Solid Professional	Playing his A-game	$15

Looking at this sample equity table, we first note that table selection is crucial to maintaining a high ROI (return on investment) for your sit 'n go's. (See "Table Selection" starting on page 235 in "Part Four: Sit 'n Go Career Play" for more on this topic). However, even a skilled table selector cannot get around the fundamental fact that:

> No player knows his own, nor any other player's, exact equity going into a tournament.

You can never sit down and say, "I will win exactly ten dollars on average playing this tournament." Each player has a different equity for that particular tournament depending on his own skills and various other factors, such as the styles and positions of his opponents.

Equity uncertainty is fundamental to tournament poker play in at least two regards:

1. **It allows you to profit.** You make your money by having a higher equity than other players, and if these players knew with complete certainty that they were losing money in the long-term with each sit 'n go they played, they would play rarely or never. You can make long-term winning investments precisely because natural fluctuations (aka luck) prevent your losing opponents from realizing that they are indeed losing.

2. **It causes vast fluctuations in your bankroll.** You will inevitably face winning and losing streaks rather than a steady bankroll climb. This may cause you to doubt your own playing ability at times, and it necessarily makes for uncertain short-term profit or loss. This is one unavoidable characteristic of poker-playing in general.

So far we have discussed only starting tournament equity. But after each action occurs, your equity will change. Our first hand analysis illustrates this point by showing how a particular hand affects the equity of each tournament participant.

Situation: It is the first hand of a $109 sit 'n go, and all fold to the hyper-aggressive blinds, Jim and Bob. They raise and reraise until all their chips are in the center pre-flop. Jim then flips

while Bob proudly shows his

Question: What happens to everyone's equity as a result?

Answer: Assuming 2♥2♣ is precisely even money with A♦K♦ (see "Appendix D: Pre-Flop Hand Probabilities" on page 257), then both will gain or lose no chips in the long run. "Therefore," one might reason, "in the long run, neither Jim nor Bob lose nor gain anything, and everyone else is unaffected by this pot."

This reasoning is flawed because chips are not money. *Doubling up early only doubles your chip count, not your equity.* Clearly you will win more money on average with an early chip double-up, but your equity will not double, it less-than-doubles. This is because chips are worth less the more you have. The loser of this race has lost chips of greater value than those the winner receives. Therefore Jim and Bob are both hurt by their early showdown, as each is risking his entire tournament equity, at even money, to less-than-double this equity. So after many sit 'n go's, both Jim and Bob place out of the money in half, and will not recover these losses by doubling-up early in the other half.

But equity does not simply disappear. There is a constant $1,000 of total equity in a 10 player $109 sit 'n go, and each player, assuming equally skilled, has a starting equity of roughly $100. Assume Bob's deuces prevail. Then Jim loses $100 in equity, Bob gains less than $100, say $90, and so the remaining $10 goes to ... the remaining players. Each gains a slight share of that $10, stemming from the fact that there is one less player who can potentially finish in the money.

So in the Jim-Bob race example, going into the flop, Jim and Bob are both long-term equity losers, and the remaining players are the long-term equity gainers.

Now suppose Bob wins with his deuces and then goes on a tear, eliminating player after player. If you simply fold every hand, so that your chip stack remains constant (ignoring the low blinds you must post in the process), you win money with each hand that passes. To be concrete:

No. of Players	Bob's Stack	Your Stack	Your Equity
10	t2,000	t2,000	$100
9	t4,000	t2,000	$102
8	t6,000	t2,000	$106
7	t8,000	t2,000	$114
6	t10,000	t2,000	$128
5	t12,000	t2,000	$150
4	t14,000	t2,000	$189
3	t16,000	t2,000	$271
2	t18,000	t2,000	$320

(These numbers were generated using a procedure called the Independent Chip Model, which is discussed further in the "Independent Chip Model (ICM)" starting on page 117 in "Part Two: Mid-Blind Play.")

So in this sample sit 'n go, you increase your equity by over 200 percent in a stretch where you do not win a single chip. This may be an exaggerated example, where only one player is gaining chips at an exorbitant rate, but the general principle holds: You gain equity (aka win money) with each opponent that gets eliminated.

Before launching into the details of low-blind sit 'n go play, we must discuss several more critical preliminary concepts. Understanding these important ideas is integral to success in any form of poker you play, be it cash seven-card stud to the no-limit sit 'n go.

Pot Odds

The single most important factor in deciding whether to call a bet is the odds offered by the pot. This is like any other investment: To know whether you should accept a certain risk, you must also know the corresponding reward. Pot odds are defined as the size of the pot (your reward) divided by the size of the bet (what you must risk).

Let us calculate the pot odds at two points during a sample hand:

The blinds are t50-t100. Two players limp. You are on the button. What are your pot odds?
Answer: The pot is t350 and the bet is t100, so your pot odds are t350-to-t100 or 3.5-to-1.

You call. The small blind folds and the big blind checks. After the flop, the first limper bets t100, and the second limper raises to t250. What are the pot odds?
Answer: The pot has t450 from the pre-flop action, t100 from the first bettor, and an extra t250 from the raiser. The total pot is t800. Meanwhile, it costs you t250 to call. Therefore, your pot odds are t800-to-t250 or 3.2-to-1.

(Note in this particular hand that the presence of the still-active first bettor requires you to have a better hand than you might otherwise call with when getting 3.2-to-1, as he may reraise putting you off the hand entirely.)

During live game play, or without software, estimating is fine, such as: "The pot is t800 and it costs me t250 to call, so I'm getting a little better than 3-to-1." If you are uncomfortable with quick mental math approximations, do not hesitate to use a calculator if playing online.

Pot odds are important because each time you wager chips, those chips are actually an investment you are making to win the pot. Pot odds tell you how good this investment is. For example, suppose you are heads-up at the river with a board of Q♣T♥8♦8♣4♠. You hold A♣4♠, and your opponent bets t200. Should you call?

Suppose the pot going into the river is t1,800. Then regardless of the prior action in this hand, you must call due simply to pot odds. This is because you are investing t200 to win t2,000 (10-to-1 pot odds). If you call and lose, you forfeit only t200, but if you call and win, you gain t2,000. This is too good a deal to pass up. Call unless you are somehow positive you are beat.

But suppose the pot going into the river was t100. Then you are investing t200 to win t300 (3-to-2 pot odds). This wager is much worse. A call and loss still costs t200, whereas now a win yields only t300. With your bottom pair you can beat only a hand such as ace-high, and so now you would only call if you thought your opponent was bluffing.

Here is a more interesting example. You are heads-up at the flop with a pot of t1,000 during t20-t40. The board is

and you hold

Your opponent min-bets t40, and you feel strongly he has the ace. Call, raise, or fold?

Answer: Call. Raising is crazy. But you should not fold. You are getting 26-to-1 pot odds, and 2 of the 46 remaining cards will improve you to a full house. So you improve to the best hand 1 in 23 times. Meanwhile, getting 26-to-1 odds, you will win chips if you make a winning hand more than 1 in 27 times. So even though you are a huge underdog at the moment, the fantastic pot odds indicate you should call this bet with a worse hand.

Furthermore, when you do improve, your opponent will probably be willing to go all-in with his trip aces, and so you stand to win considerably more. This concept is called *implied odds,* a term originally coined by David Sklansky. You are risking chips to win not only what is currently in the pot, but what you expect the pot to be after future betting rounds as well.

Implied odds are a crucial concept in cash no-limit hold 'em, but for our purposes, it suffices to realize implied odds give the justification for playing the speculative hands we will discuss. When you call behind a chain of limpers pre-flop during low-blind play with low suited connectors, you are hoping to win more than the measly pre-flop bets when you hit a monster. It is the many chips you hope to win in later betting rounds, the implied odds, that make such speculative pre-flop calls well worth it.

Chip Expected Value

Assessing how many chips you figure to win or lose by making a particular play is key to determining whether this play is positive equity. This assessment is known as "Chip Expected Value."

The expected value (EV) of a wager is how much it wins you on average. It is calculated by weighting each possible outcome with how likely it is to occur.

For instance, if you bet $1 at even money that a normal coin will land heads, you have an EV of zero:

$$EV = \left(\text{probability of landing heads}\right)\left(\$ \text{ you win if heads lands}\right)$$
$$+ \left(\text{probability of landing tails}\right)\left(\$ \text{ you lose if tails lands}\right)$$

$$= \left(.5\right)\left(\$1\right) + \left(.5\right)\left(-1\right) = \$0$$

Now suppose you are offered 3-to-1 odds that the roll of a die will land on 4. You accept the wager and bet $2. What is the EV of this gamble?

Answer: -$0.67. The die will land on four 1 in 6 times. Getting 3-to-1 means you will get paid 3 times what you bet if you win, or $6. Meanwhile, the other five-sixths of the time the die will land on a different number, and you will lose the $2 you wagered.

So the expected value is a loss of 67 cents:

$$-\$0.666 = \left(\frac{1}{6}\right)(\$6) + \left(\frac{5}{6}\right)(-\$2)$$

In cash poker, the expected value of a move is the amount of money it will make or lose for you on average. This is no different than equity for cash play.

But in tournament poker, winning chips and winning money are different.

Equity: The amount of money a play will make in the long run.

Chip Expected Value (cEV): The number of chips a play will make in the long run. (The "c" is placed before EV to indicate that we are discussing expected value in chips rather than money terms.)

Here is an example of a cEV calculation. You hold

and the flop is

The pot is t1,000, and your lone opponent goes all-in for another t400. Will calling earn you chips in the long run?

Answer: Yes. This question may be rephrased to read, "Does calling have a cEV that is positive?" So let us calculate the cEV of the call. Assume you make your straight exactly one-third of the time. (You may find all such probabilities in "Appendix C: Drawing Odds Chart" starting on page 253.)

So two-thirds of the time you will lose the hand, costing you t400. The other one-third of the time, you will win the t400 he bet, plus the t1,000 already in the pot, for a total of t1,400. Therefore if you call your expectation is t200 (in chips).

$$t200 = \left(\frac{1}{3}\right)(t1,400) + \left(\frac{2}{3}\right)(-t400)$$

So calling will indeed earn chips in the long run.

If you fold, you automatically win or lose no more chips, and so the cEV of a fold is 0. It does not matter if you already invested half your stack into the pot; this was a prior action, and the cEV of a move is independent of anything that occurred earlier in the hand or tournament. You may have made a bad play to be in the situation, but prior actions obviously cannot be changed. So the fold option always wins exactly 0 chips.

The Aggression Principle

Whenever you play poker, you need a stronger hand to call than you would to bet or raise. This is because betting and raising allow the possibility of winning the pot immediately as everyone may fold. But you can never win immediately by calling.

This principle was formulated as the "Gap Concept" by David Sklansky (see *Tournament Poker for Advanced Players*). We will talk in greater detail about the gap between hands good enough to be the caller rather than the bettor in the mid- and high-blind sections. For now, simply observe that you should make a habit of being the aggressor, which brings us to "The Aggression Principle."

> Being the bettor/raiser is better than being the caller. This is because betting and raising allow the possibility of winning the pot immediately since everyone may fold. But you can never win immediately by calling.

Make sure you are comfortable with this idea as it is one of the most crucial observations in all of poker.

Hands to Play
During Low Blinds

There are three types of hands that should be played by any sit 'n go player during low-blind play. These are:

1. **Premium Hands:** Monsters such as

and

2. **Speculative Hands:** Hands with great post-flop potential, such as 4♥4♣ or 8♠7♠, when you expect to see a cheap flop against many opponents.

3. **Late Position "Steal" Hands:** Solid hands in late position, such as

on the button, which will often win a small uncontested pot, and have potential to solidly connect with the flop if called.

These hand categories are all sufficiently strong that regardless of your experience and playing ability, they will be profitable in the long run.

Premium Hands

No matter how low the blinds, you will always want to play the monster hands: AA, KK, QQ, and AK.

Pocket Aces through Queens

Raise or reraise big before the flop with these hands, particularly in the low stakes sit 'n go's. Your raise is important both as a value bet (betting with what you believe to be the best hand for the purpose of accumulating chips), and to limit the number of opponents.

Ideally, you want to take down a sizeable pot before the flop, particularly with queens. If there has been a lot of raising pre-flop, you might limp from early position, reraising a raiser, and folding post-flop if many players see the flop without a raise and you miss your set.

If you do get callers to a raise or reraise, and an ace or king comes to your queens or an ace to your kings, tend to give up against multiple opponents or a lot of action. These are all cards your opponents are likely to have, and you would like them to show weakness by all checking at least once before you make a move. Against few opponents showing weakness, ignore the overcard and bet around half the pot.

If your pre-flop raise gets many callers and there is a lot of action post-flop, and/or the board is dangerous (such as

and you are holding two black aces facing a bet and two smooth calls), you should not hesitate to discard aces or kings after the flop.

If you are the aggressor, you should always be willing to go all-in before the flop with a high pocket pair. Having such a hand and being the pre-flop aggressor is one time you should always be willing to play a big pot during low-blind play.

Now suppose you are not the aggressor. If an opponent puts you all-in pre-flop, always call with aces or kings. But depending on the action, you may have to lay down queens. (See the hand examples below.) This is because all-ins during Levels 1 and 2 require you to have a clear chip advantage if you are the caller.

Most sections of this book will consist of text followed by hand examples. In the examples where players are denoted by position, the following abbreviations are used, starting with the player one to the left of the big blind: Under-the-gun (UTG), UTG+1, UTG+2, MP1, MP2, and MP3 (also called the hijack seat). The cutoff seat, button, small blind, and big blind will always be written out. However, BB will sometimes be used to denote how many bets you have in terms of big blinds

The number in parenthesis following a player is his chip count. If the player is the small or big blind, this parenthetical number is his remaining chip count after posting this blind. (Hands where the suits of the cards are not explicitly given are labeled "s" for suited and "o" for offsuit. Thus ace-king suited may be A♦K♦, A♠K♠, A♣K♣, or A♥K♥, or AKs, and AKo represents any of the twelve other ace-kings.)

The common playing style categories are abbreviated as follows: tight-aggressive (TAG), loose-aggressive (LAG), tight-passive (TP), loose-passive (LP).

Some hands will supply more information about your opponents than others. This is because information that is crucial in one hand may be insignificant or unknown in another, such as an early versus middle position limper or the playing style of your opponent, and the examples here are designed to reflect this fact.

As a corollary, you should be able to classify your opponents' playing styles with roughly the frequency found in this text. Learning how to label your opponents' styles is a crucial skill and is discussed in detail in the section "Hand Reading Skills" starting on page 225 in "Part Four: Sit 'n Go Career Play." There is also software that automatically tracks your opponents' play, which is discussed in "Software" starting on page 232 in "Part Four: Sit 'n Go Career Play."

Hand 1-1

Blinds: t20-t40; 10 players

Your hand: You (t1,940) have Q♠Q♣ in MP1.
Action to you: UTG (t1,820) opens for t100. The next two players fold.

Question: What is your move?
> **Answer:** Raise to about t350. You want to win the pot immediately, or limit the field to at most one or two opponents. Make a solid raise.

Action: You raise to t350, everyone to your left folds to the tight-aggressive big blind (t1,940) who pushes all-in. UTG calls.

Question: Call or fold?

Answer: Fold. Low-blind pre-flop all-ins are very consistent with aces or kings. Against a single opponent, particularly a low-stakes loose player, the odds of him holding a lesser hand (ideally jacks or ace-queen suited, leaving you a heavy favorite) may make a call worthwhile. But after a raise and a reraise, a tight opponent reraises for all his chips, and gets called. It is very likely you are up against aces or kings, and despite having an excellent hand pre-flop, you must fold. You should also fold ace-king in this situation. Only call here with aces or kings.

Hand 1-2

Blinds: t20-t40, 9 players

Your hand: You (t1,940) have K♠K♣ under-the-gun. The table has been generally loose with most hands seeing a pre-flop raiser and many callers.

Question: What is your play?

Answer: Call t40. Being early to act against a loose table, call with the intention of reraising a raiser. Raising yourself is a reasonable option, but with a high pocket pair in early position at a loose table, your best chance of winning a big pot pre-flop is to call and hope for a raise. If it doesn't come, you can easily get away from a bad flop since the pot will be small.

Action: You call t40, triggering five more calls and a check from the big blind. (There are seven players and t280 in the pot.)

Flop: Q♥Q♣T♦
Action: The blinds check.

Question: Check or bet?
Answer: Check. The unraised pot is not a large one, and it is too likely one of your six opponents has a queen, in which case you are drawing dead to a king — about an 8 percent longshot. If everyone checks behind you, you may bet the turn so long as it is not an ace or ten (giving anyone with either of these cards a better hand).

Action: The player to your left bets t40, and gets three callers.

Question: Call, raise, or fold?
  Answer: Call. You may be beat, but the pot is t440, so you are getting 11-to-1. Your call closes the action, so there cannot be a raise. Meanwhile, should you turn a king (23-to-1 against), expect to take down a monster pot against an opponent with trip queens. It is also possible your hand is best.

Action: You call. (There are five players and t480 in the pot.)

Turn: 3♦

Action: The small blind bets t250

Question: Call, raise, or fold?
  Answer: Fold. This is an unusual bet, and you may well have the small blind beat. This is because he would probably check a queen as he did on the flop. However, there are still three active players left, any one of whom might call or raise if you stick around. Give it up now.

(While many of the hand examples in this section continue post-flop, so play after the flop will be discussed systematically in the next section. For now, make sure you understand the pre-flop concepts, and treat the post-flop material as an introduction to the topic.)

Ace-King

This is a great hand for low-blind play. It is less dangerous than a high pocket pair since you may easily let it go at the flop if you miss, and if you hit, the ace or king that must land makes for one less card that can help an opponent.

Suppose, for instance, you hold

and the flop comes

Then you would face a tough decision against heavy action since your overpair is strong but the coordinated board may already have you beat. But you would have an easy fold with since the board would have to fall with an ace or king instead of one of the low straight flush cards for you to have a hand.

Tend to make a standard raise of roughly 3BB (big blinds, so in t25-t50, 3BB = t150) if you are first to enter, and add a bit more for each limper. For instance, if the blinds are t20-t40 and you have ace-king on the button facing three limpers, raise to t175 or so. If the pot has already been raised, often just call so as to avoid playing a large pot post-flop during low-blind play before you have a clear idea of where you stand. If there has already been a raise and several callers, so that the pot is already large and worth winning, you can avoid the post-flop dilemma by simply raising all-in pre-flop.

At the flop, bet for value if you hit your ace or king. This bet should be higher with more opponents and more coordinated boards that allow draws. If you miss, usually make a continuation bet of one-half to two-thirds of the pot if you were the pre-flop aggressor and everyone shows weakness by checking at least once.

Hand 1-3

Blinds: t30-t60, 9 players

Your hand: You (t1,940) have A♠K♣ in the cut-off.
Action to you: A loose player (t2,200) raises to t120 from MP1, everyone else folds

Question: Fold, call, or raise?

    Answer: Call. You want to minimize early swings in your chip stack, and so with ace-king, often call a raise, rather than reraise, during low-blind play.

Action: You call, as do the button and both blinds. (There are five players and t600 in the pot.)

Flop: Q♠T♣2♥
Action: The blinds checks, and the initial raiser bets t200.

Question: What is your play?

    Answer: Fold. You largely missed the flop. Your only certain outs are the 4 jacks, as an ace or king may make an opponent's straight or two pair. Furthermore, you are one to the left of the bettor. Even if you have him beat, there are two active players left behind who may be intending to call with a better hand, or make a raise you cannot call.

In the above hand, reraising pre-flop would hardly be unreasonable. But now let us consider a low-blind ace-king situation where raising is the manifestly superior play.

Hand 1-4

Blinds: t30-t60, 9 players

Your hand: You (t1,940) have A♠K♣ in the small blind.
Action to you: A loose player (t2,200) raises to t200 from MP1. The cutoff ($2,100) and button ($1,760) both smooth-call.

Question: Fold, call, or raise?

    Answer: Push all-in. Your hand is an excellent move-in hand as you are only a huge underdog to pocket aces and 30 percent against kings, and there is already t690 in the pot. Make an aggressive play to increase your stack by one-third.

Another way to analyze your options is via process of elimination: Your hand is too strong to fold, and if you call, you will have the worst position in all subsequent betting rounds against three or four opponents. This makes raising all-in clearly the superior play.

Action: You raise all-in and all fold to the button. He pauses substantially before calling, showing 6♠6♣.

While you would have preferred everyone to fold, your coin-flip for all your chips is subsidized by nearly t500 in dead money, making this a fine situation. If you do not spike an ace or king, move on to the next sit 'n go knowing you made the correct play.

Ace-Queen, Ace-Jack Suited, Jacks Down Through Nines

These are solid, but not premium hands. Do not usually get involved with ace-queen offsuit or any ace-jack in early position. Limp or make a standard raise with AQs, 99, and TT, and raise with jacks.

In middle or late position, call or raise with all these hands against limpers/folders, but tend to fold (particularly ace-queen offsuit and nines) if someone has raised already. This is because if the raiser has a better hand (such as ace-king if you have ace-queen, or jacks if you have nines), you will often lose all your chips on a seemingly favorable flop.

Hand 1-5

Blinds: t30-t60, 10 players

Your hand: You (t1,850) have 9♠9♣ in the small blind.
Action to you: One player (t1,720) limps from middle position. Everyone else folds.

Question: Fold, call, or raise?
    Answer: Call. If you do raise, you must raise big (to t300 or so) to discourage action since you will act first on each betting round. I prefer calling since the pot is small and a raise that does not win immediately makes for a difficult situation. Here, if you hit the nine, golden. If the flop comes three low cards, you still have an excellent hand. And against overcards, you may quietly leave the pot.

Action: You call, and the loose-passive big blind (t2,100) checks. (There are three players and t180 in the pot.)

Flop: J♣6♠2♠

Question: Check or bet?
    Answer: Check. Betting is not unreasonable. But the pot is small, and if your opponents do not retreat from a bet, you will be out of position in a hand where the big blind or limper could easily hold a jack. If both players check, bet the turn (t100 or so) if it comes a blank (in this case, a low non-spade).

Action: You check, the big blind checks, and the limper bets t90.

Question: Call or fold?
    Answer: Fold. You are getting decent odds (3-to-1) with what may be the best hand, but the pot is small, you are

unlikely to improve if beaten, and the big blind could still raise. Get out now.

Hand 1-6

Blinds: t30-t60, 10 players

Your hand: You (t1,830) have A♠J♣ in the hijack seat.
Action to you: All fold to your loose rightmost opponent (t2,200) who raises to t140.

Question: What is your move?
Answer: Fold.

Let's discuss the three options in turn.

- **Reraise:** This is an aggressive play, but not an optimal one. You should never look to play large pots with marginal hands during low blinds. If you get reraised back, either by the initial raiser or another active opponent, you must fold. If you get called, you will still lose all your chips at the flop if you make your hand and your opponent has you beat (namely with ace-king or ace-queen). Even if everyone folds and you win the pot pre-flop, an extra t210, while helpful, is not worth the risk.

- **Call:** The call allows you to see a flop with a good hand if no remaining opponent raises, nor are you over-committing yourself. The problem is that ace-jack is a dangerous hand post-flop. If your opponent has ace-queen or ace-king (and both of these hands would be consistent with his pre-flop play), you will lose many chips if an ace hits. Indeed, this is often how weaker players get eliminated in ninth or tenth — playing and hitting a hand that proves second best. A flop of two low cards and a jack would give you a strong hand, but should your opponent be holding an unlikely overpair, you figure to lose all your chips. Avoid these marginal situations during low-blind play.

- **Fold:** By process of elimination, you should fold. Ace-jack is a good hand when you are short-stacked relative to the blinds, or if you are the initial raiser in middle or late position. When the blinds are small and there has been action before you, however, or you are in early position, get in the habit of laying down ace-jack and ace-queen and save yourself the ninth and tenth place finishes.

Hand 1-7

Blinds: t20-t40, 10 players

Your hand: You (t2,000) have J♠J♣ in MP1.
Action to you: Everyone folds.

Question: What is your move?
　　Answer: Raise to about t140. This raise is both for value and to limit the number of opponents to at most one or two.

Action: You raise to t140. All fold to the loose big blind (t2,360) who calls for t100. (There are two players and t300 in the pot.)

Flop: 7♣5♣5♠
Action: The big blind bets t240.

Question: Fold, call, or raise?
　　Answer: Raise t600. When you show strength pre-flop, and your opponent bets out at the flop, he rarely has a strong hand. For if he did, he would check and let you bet. Even very beginning players seem to understand this principle, and

would slow-play trip fives in this scenario. Similarly, with QQ – AA, he would almost certainly have reraised pre-flop,[2] or if not, checked the flop and waited for your bet to raise. Likely holdings for your opponent are a pair of sevens (such as king-seven suited or ace-seven), or a low pocket pair (such as 4♦4♥). Your high overpair figures to be the best hand, and the t540 pot is significant, so raise now.

Action: You raise to t600. He calls. (There are two players and t1,500 in the pot.)

Turn: 2♠
Action: Your opponent checks.

Question: Do you check or bet?
  Answer: Push all-in. The pot is huge — larger even than your t1,260 remaining stack, and you are very likely to have the best hand. You must be cautious during low-blind play, but do not give up on what figures to be the best hand when you are the aggressor in a huge heads-up pot.
  Note that a smaller bet is unnecessary when the pot is so large. In addition, many river cards could demote your hand to second best (most notably a seven or any club), so you must make your opponent pay the maximum to draw.

Speculative Hands

Playable speculative hands are those satisfying three conditions:

---

[2] It should be mentioned that against the better players in the high stakes sit 'n go's this whole line of play is more debatable. You may well be up against a big hand. But I did specify that in this case the big blind was loose.

1. You are in middle or late position.

2. The pot is unraised and there are at least two limpers. And,

3. You are holding a hand which could develop into a post-flop monster.

Condition No. 3 — the speculative component —- usually means suited connectors (five-four suited and up), suited aces (such as A♠4♠), or ideally, a low-mid pocket pair. Mid- high-suited semi-connectors (such as J♣9♣ s or K♦T♦) also qualify in late position after several limpers. Your goal is to see a cheap flop, quietly mucking your cards to an unfavorable flop (as is probable), or winning a large pot if you flop a monster or huge draw against many opponents.

If the pots are usually unraised pre-flop, limp with all low pocket pairs from any position during low blinds especially if there is already at least one caller.

Important: Do *not* use speculative hands to justify playing trash hands or calling big pre-flop raises. For instance, if you are in late position after several limpers, but your hand is

or

fold. If you are in late position with

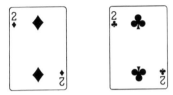

and three players are already in the pot, but the opener raised from t60 to t200, fold.

Also, be less inclined to play your hand if you think there is an above-average chance a player yet to act will raise, such as a reckless short-stacked opponent seated in the big blind.

Hand 1-8

Blinds: t30-t60, 9 players

Your hand: You (t1,940) are MP3 with 5♠5♣. Play has been very loose.

Action to you: Three of the first five players limp.

Question: What is your play?
> **Answer:** Call. While you are not in late position, the implied odds are too good to pass up. You will know right where you stand at the flop. If a five does not hit, simply check/fold your hand (unless the flop is something like 4♣3♠2♥).

Hand 1-9

Blinds: t20-t40, 10 players

Your hand: You (t2,040) have A♠4♠ on the button.

Action to you: Two players (t1,860 and t2,000) limp. The small blind (t1,900) is tight-aggressive, and you know nothing about your remaining opponents.

Question: What is your move?

>   **Answer:** Call with this suited ace on the button as a speculative low-blind hand.

Action: You call. The small blind calls and the big blind checks. (There are five players and t200 in the pot.)

Flop: A♥T♣8♠

Action: Everyone checks to you.

Question: What do you do?

>   **Answer:** Bet t120. You have top pair with a backdoor flush draw, and everyone has shown weakness.

Action: You bet. The big blind folds. The TAG small blind and initial limper call. The second limper folds. (There are three players and t560 in the pot.)

Turn: 6♠

Action: It is checked to you.

Question: Do you check or bet?

>   **Answer:** Check. You got called in two spots with your bet on the raggedy flop, and so another bet is unlikely to win right here. Furthermore, you have picked up a draw to the nut flush. So take your free card rather than risk a raise.

River: Q♦

Action: The small blind bets t400, and the limper calls.

Question: Call or fold?
    Answer: Fold. This is a large bet made by a TAG player during low-blind play against two opponents. He almost certainly isn't bluffing, and the call by your unknown opponent cements this into a clear fold with your now weak top pair hand.

Hand 1-10

Blinds: t20-t40, 10 players

Your hand: You (t1,940) have 5♠4♠ on the button.
Action to you: Four players call before the cut-off doubles to t80.

Question: What is your move?
    Answer: Fold. You have a quality speculative hand in position, but the cutoff's raise opens betting back up to the original limpers, any one of whom could reraise.

Late Position Value Hands

A low-blind hand worth playing for value should satisfy three criteria:

1.   You have a decent hand in late position.

2.   Everyone has folded up to you. And,

3.   You think a raise is likely to win the pot uncontested.

As with speculative hands, neither of these factors is enough individually to ensure positive equity. For instance, if you are on the button at t20-t40 with

do not raise against one limper and a LAG big blind. If everyone folds you win a small pot, but you will often be called, putting yourself in a position to play a larger pot with a non-premium hand during low-blind play.

Now suppose you have J♣7♦ on the cutoff in an unopened pot with only tight players remaining, fold again. Your hand is weak, and the reward for stealing not sufficient. But with king-ten suited instead of jack-seven offsuit, you should play. You will usually win a small pot immediately. But even if you happen to get called in two places (indicating you are likely to be facing a better hand), you may still win a big pot if you catch a straight, flush, or high two pair.

If the flop misses you, tend to make a half-pot continuation bet if all appear weak. But if someone raises or bets before you act put no more money into the pot.

Hand 1-11

Blinds: t30-t60, 9 players

Your hand: You (t1,940) have 8♠8♣ in MP3.
Action to you: Everyone folds.

Question: What is your move?
    Answer: Raise to t180. You have a good hand relatively late to act in an unopened pot, a situation meriting a raise.

Action: You raise to t180 and are called only by the loose-passive big blind (t2,100). (There are two active players and t390 in the pot.)

Flop: 7♠6♣2♣
Action: Your opponent checks.

Question: Check or bet?
    Answer: Bet t350. With your overpair (and backdoor straight draw), you almost certainly have the best hand, yet it is a vulnerable one. Protect it with a pot-sized bet.

Action: You bet t350, and he calls. (There is t1,090 in the pot.)

Turn: A♦
Action: He checks again.

Question: Check or bet?
    Answer: Bet t400. This bet has two purposes.

1. You may win a pot you would otherwise lose. If your opponent is playing random high cards excluding the ace, he may fold now rather than pay to draw to a pair above yours.

2. While many loose opponents will play dubious aces, your eights will usually prevail at showdown in a heads-up situation. By making a bet here, you likely buy yourself a free showdown. If you check, your opponent may well bet the river after your display of weakness. This will put you in a difficult situation. Rather than

choose between folding and calling at the river, simply bet the turn instead.

Since your opponent is passive, you may safely lay down your hand against a turn raise, as you are almost certainly up against a better hand (usually ace-x). Note that if your opponent is aggressive, checking becomes a reasonable option to induce a bluff on the river.

Hand 1-12

Blinds: t20-t40, 9 players

Your hand: You (t1,820) have K♠T♦ on the button.
Action to you: Everyone folds.

Question: What is your move?
   Answer: Raise to t120. This is a good low-blind steal, as you have a decent hand in late position in an unopened pot.

Now suppose in the above hand two players limp from early positions. Then you should fold since king-ten offsuit no longer has steal potential. But consider smooth-calling with king-ten suited as a speculative hand.

Hand 1-13

Blinds: t30-t60, 10 players

Your hand: You (t1,800) have 9♦9♥ in the cut-off seat. Play has been generally tight. The big blind seems tight-passive.
Action to you: Everyone folds.

Question: What is your move?

Answer: Raise to t180. Nines is a solid holding in late position against few opponents, and the big blind is tight. This combination makes this a classic low-blind late position steal hand. You are looking to take the t90 on the table or win a small pot after the flop.

Action: You raise to t180. The button and small blind fold. The big blind (t1,400) calls another t120. (There are two players and t390 in the pot.)

Flop: Q♠8♣4♥

Action: The big blind checks.

Question: Check or bet?

Answer: Bet t200. The odds are good this flop missed your opponent, and since he is passive, his check is most likely literal. A bet of half the pot will often take it right here. Note that betting a larger, pot-sized amount is unnecessary. If your opponent will call t200, he will most likely call t400.

Action: You bet t200. The big blind calls. (There is t790 in the pot.)

Turn: 9♣

Action: The big blind checks.

Question: Check or bet?

Answer: Bet t450. It is almost certain you have the best hand. A tight opponent would not call your flop bet with only a gutshot draw (which a straight-making jack-ten would be at the flop). His most likely holdings are ace-eight suited or any queen. But with straight and flush draws on board, you cannot take that chance and offer him a free card. You want to get value for your quality hand. If he folds, fine. The pot is large, and your hand, while excellent, is not unbeatable.

Post-Flop Low-Blind Play

Let us categorize post-flop low-blind play into four categories:

1. **Excellent Flops:** These are hands where you flop top pair, top kicker, or better.

2. **Solid Draws:** Hands where you flop a draw to the nut flush, mid pair plus an open-ended straight draw or flush draw, or other quality draw.

3. **Hands where you were the pre-flop aggressor but miss:** For instance, you raise pre-flop with A♠K♥, get called, and the flop comes three low cards.

4. **Marginal Hands:** Hands where you flop a weak top pair or other modest hand.

All other hands where you are neither the pre-flop aggressor nor have a piece of the flop should tend to be check/folded.

Excellent Flops

If you raise pre-flop with a premium holding and flop a hand such as top pair, top kicker, or an overpair to the board, you should exploit your opponents' looseness and bet for value relentlessly. Bet more with more opponents and more dangerous boards. You want to force your opponents to choose between making an unprofitable call or simply surrendering the pot without a fight.

Hand 1-14

Blinds: t30-t60, 9 players

Your hand: You (t2,000) have A♠K♣ in MP3.
Action to you: Two players limp and you raise to t200. Both
   blinds fold. The first limper (t2,020) calls, and the second
   limper folds. (There are two players and t550 in the pot.)

Flop: K♥8♠2♦
Action: Your opponent checks.

Question: Check or bet?
   Answer: Bet t200. With a single opponent and ragged board,
   bet for value on the smaller side. This is because there are
   very few turn cards that have the potential to devalue your
   hand — no flush draws, no straight draws, and so forth.
   Therefore your bet with top pair, top kicker is purely for
   value. If the flop were instead K♠9♥8♥, or a board allowing
   more draws, you should bet a larger amount.

Action: You bet t200, and he calls. (There are two players and
   t950 in the pot.)

Turn: 7♦
Action: He checks.

Question: Check or bet?
   Answer: Bet t500, again for value.

Action: You bet t500 and he raises all-in.

Question: Call or fold?
   Answer: Call. Going into the turn, you had t1,600, and he
   had you covered. So the pot is t950 + t500 + t1,600 = t3,050,

and it costs you t1,100 to call. So you are getting between 2.5-to-1 and 3-to-1, while holding top pair, top kicker. It is possible you are beat at the moment (against a set of deuces in particular), but you cannot lay down such a strong hand against a single opponent in a huge pot offering good odds.

Now let us modify the above problem such that your pre-flop raise to t200 with A♠K♣ was called by the second limper (t2,380) as well, and the flop came more dangerous than before. (There are three active players and t690 in the pot.)

Flop: K♥T♣9♥
Action: The limpers check.

Question: Check or bet?
> **Answer:** Bet t500. With two opponents and a dangerous board, you need to make a big bet so that those drawing to a straight or flush cannot profitably call. You are happy to take the pot right here, and if you get called and the turn comes a blank, be prepared to get all your chips in. Should you be reraised all-in, you may have to fold, particularly against a loose opponent.

Action: You bet t500 and one of your opponents smooth-calls. (There are two players and t1,690 in the pot.)

Turn: J♥
Action: He bets t60.

Question: Fold, call, or raise?
> **Answer:** Call. Consider hands your opponent could reasonably have after his pre-flop and flop calls: AQ, KQ, KJ, KT, JJ-99, QJ, JTs, QTs, or A♥X♥. Each of these hands is now a straight, flush, or two pair. Any other hand, such as 88 or AT, would indicate a recklessly loose call post-flop. If

you are playing against a reckless low-stakes opponent, and would therefore be willing to call an all-in should he push here, then you should push yourself. But against a normal opponent, even a loose one, just call — you cannot fold top pair getting nearly 30-to-1 pot odds, after all — and see what he does on the river.

Action: You call. (There are two players and t1,810 in the pot.)

River: 2♣
Action: He pushes all-in.

Question: Call or fold?

    Answer: Fold. You have t1,240 left, and the pot is t1,810 + t1,240 = t3,050. Getting 5-to-2, you should tend to call if you believe your winning chances are better than 2 in 7. With four high cards to a straight, a 3-flush, and many two-pair possibilities, coupled with your opponent's actions, you winning chances are slim indeed. Furthermore, with t1,240 left, and the blinds only t30-t60, you still have a respectable amount of equity if you fold. Walk away from this one.

The above hands concerned excellent flops, but some consideration should be given to monster flops as well, such as hitting a straight or flush.

    If you flop a vulnerable monster, such as

on a flop of

or 5♣4♣ on a flop of Q♣9♣7♣, push hard at the flop. Your goal when flopping a vulnerable monster is to either take down whatever's on the table, or get an inferior hand to pay more than it is worth to see another card. If the pot is large, tend to bet or raise big regardless of your position. If the pot is small, bet or raise a pot-sized amount. If you get one or more callers and the turn is bad (such as a jack in the straight example or a fourth club in the flush example), play cautiously. Fold if you are unsure, particularly in a smaller pot with a lot of action.

You may want to take it slow with a monster unlikely to be outdrawn, such as the nut straight on a rainbow flop, the nut flush, or a full house. If you are checked to in late position and were the pre-flop aggressor, make a small bet (half the pot or under) for value. If you decide to check in early position and nobody bets, you must bet the turn. You need value for your strong hands.

Realize that very few hands are unbeatable after the flop. For instance,

on a flop of

is a very solid hand. Yet it is not invincible. If one of the six remaining aces or kings hits (which it will 25 percent of the time), you may have to settle for half the pot. If another queen, jack, or ten falls, you may lose to a full house. And over 12 percent of the time a club, spade, or heart flush will be possible by the river. So if your value bet chases everyone away, that is far from disastrous.

But your opponents will often give you plenty of action if you bet early, even if no one improves to beat you. Checking early may simply result in winning a smaller pot than if you had value-bet each street. This is particularly true when your opponent is on a draw and therefore cannot call a river bet if he misses.

Hand 1-15

Blinds: t20-t40, 10 players

Your hand: You (t1,960) have 2♥2♣ in the big blind.
Action to you: There are four limpers. The small blind completes. You check. (There are six players and t240 in the pot.)

Flop: 3♣3♦2♠
Action: The small blind checks.

Question: Check or bet?
> **Answer:** Check. With a monster hand where you have the low-card board monopolized, such as here, let someone else bet or wait until the turn so anyone who pairs fourth street may give you action.

Action: Everyone else checks.

Turn: 8♦
Action: The small blind checks.

Question: Check or bet?
Answer: Bet t150. This is a value bet which may be called with a variety of inferior hands, but there are two additional reasons you must bet now:

1. If everyone checks, there are five river cards that would be disastrous for you: the two remaining treys would give anyone with an eight or a pocket pair a better full house, as would a trey or an eight should another eight fall. So you must charge anyone with one of these cards to attempt to draw out on you (even though if you check someone holding one of these cards might bet anyway).

2. If anyone has picked up a diamond draw he will probably call a bet here. Then if the river is a diamond, it will be particularly hard for him to escape the hand without losing all his chips. If the river isn't a diamond, then this opponent will only lose chips if you bet on fourth street before he misses his draw.

> If you believe your opponent is on a draw on fourth street, you must bet even if your hand is unbeatable.

This is because if he misses on the river, you will not win any more chips from him (unless he happens to bluff).

Action: You bet t150. The button and small blind call. (There are three players and t690 in the pot.)

River: A♦
Action: The small blind checks.

Question: How much do you bet?
    Answer: Bet about t450. The small blind may have hit a straight with a five-four, or have been slowplaying a trey. The button may have paired his ace, and either could have hit a backdoor flush. Regardless, you should make a sizeable bet to get value for your monster hand.

Action: You bet t450 and everyone folds.

Note one more important aspect of this hand. On fourth street, a flush or straight-drawing opponent was drawing dead to your full house. Making his hand would have been terrible for him since it would still be second-best and he would probably lose all his chips.

Conversely, try not to let this happen to you. If you are in a multi-way pot and the hand you are drawing to may already be beat, realize that your draw is severely devalued since you may hit your draw yet still lose most or all of your chips in the process.

Solid Draws

Suppose you flop a flush draw or open-ended straight draw in a multi-way pot. If you are last to act and no one bets before you, tend to take the free card unless you feel that a bet has a strong chance to win immediately. This way, you are keeping the pot small, and you do not risk a raise that will force you to discard a hand that might improve to a monster by showdown.

If there are acting opponents left after you, and your draw is strong enough that you would have to call a bet were one made, tend to bet yourself so you may win the pot immediately if everyone folds. This play is a semi-bluff. You may win uncontested at the flop, or if you are called, your hand may improve to beat the caller's hand on a later street. Should an opponent raise, tend to fold unless the odds are right.

Now suppose someone bets before you. If the player to your right bets in a multi-way pot, tend to fold unless the bet is small, as any active opponent may raise, forcing you to abandon your hand. Indeed, if there is any substantial betting and raising, tend to fold unless your draw is a monster (such as the coveted open-ended straight flush draw which is the favorite over a hand as strong as an overpair to the board). With a draw this strong, tend to smooth-call in a multi-way pot, but reraise heads-up since you may win the pot immediately, and if not you may still be the favorite.

Hand 1-16

Blinds: t30-t60, 9 players

Your hand: You (t1,750) have K♥T♥ in the big blind.
Action to you: One loose-passive player (t2,100) limps in middle position. The small blind (t2,565) completes. You check. (There are three players and t180 in the pot.)

Flop: Q♣J♠5♥
Action: The small blind checks.

Question: Check or bet?
> **Answer:** Bet t100. You have an open-ended straight draw, a backdoor flush draw, and possibly the remaining kings as outs. This leaves you with approximately 11 outs. So bet this strong draw and hope to take the pot immediately. If you get called, you will improve over 20 percent of the time with each card. But against any very big raise, fold rather than play a large pot this early in the tournament.

Action: You bet t100. The limper folds. The small blind calls. (There are two players and t380 in the pot.)

Turn: 2♦
Action: The small blind checks.

Question: Check or bet?
> **Answer:** Check. You do not want to pot-commit yourself on a follow-up semi-bluff during low-blind play. If your opponent called the flop, it is unlikely he will fold to a turn blank. If you bet and he makes a sizeable raise, you will have to leave the hand. So check and take the free card.

River: A♣
Action: Your opponent checks.

Question: What is your play?
> **Answer:** Bet at least t250. Jackpot, you got your free card, leaving you with the nuts. And furthermore, loose-passive players will often stick around with any ace, so value bet aggressively as he will certainly not fold top pair in this spot, and often call with second or third pair as well.

Hand 1-17

Blinds: t20-t40, 7 players

Your hand: You (t1,960) have 7♣5♠ in the big blind.
Action to you: All fold to the button (t1,860) who calls, as does the small blind (t1,940). You check. (There are three players and t120 in the pot.)

Flop: J♥4♦2♠
Action: The small blind checks.

Question: Check or bet?
>**Answer:** Check. You have no hand and the pot is small.

Action: The button checks.

Turn: 6♥
Action: The small blind checks.

Question: Check or bet?
>**Answer:** Bet t80. Semi-bluff this small pot with your open-ended straight draw. No one has shown strength, so often you will take the pot right here. (Fold to a large raise, and if called, only play the river if you make your hand.) You have a quality draw against opponents showing weakness, and will often take the pot with little risk by making a small to moderate bet.

Hand 1-18

Blinds: t30-t60, 9 players

Your hand: You (t1,900) have A♠3♠ in the small blind. Play has been passive.
Action to you: There are two limpers (t1,800 and t2,100).

Question: Fold or call?
>**Answer:** Call. You are late to act before the flop and are being offered a discounted price with a quality speculative hand.

Action: You call and the big blind checks. (There are four players and t240 in the pot.)

Flop: J♠6♣2♠

Question: What is your move?

    Answer: Bet out. The blinds are low, but even so, your nut flush draw is too strong to fold to a bet. Therefore you should bet yourself, around around half the pot, or t120 seems about right. If everyone folds, excellent. If one or more players call, tend to check/fold if you do not improve but bet again if you make your flush. Also fold to big flop raises. Only if you are getting good odds to continue when someone plays back at you before you make your flush should you continue. Otherwise you risk becoming pot-committed during low-blind play without a solid made hand, a situation to avoid.

Action: The big blind (t2,800) and first limper (t1,650) call. The second limper folds. (There are three players and t600 in the pot.)

Turn: 8♥

Action: You check. The big blind bets t200. The limper calls.

Question: What is your move?

    Answer: The pot has t1,000 and it is t200 to call, so you are getting 5-to-1 pot odds. As you are 4-to-1 to make your flush (probably winning even more chips if you do), and your call closes the action, you should call. If you miss, you walk away from the hand having lost about t400, leaving you in decent shape as the blinds are still low. But if you catch a spade, you win a large pot.

Hand 1-19

Blinds: t30-t60, 9 players

Your hand: You (t1,820) have T♠9♠ in the big blind.
Action to you: UTG min-raises to t120 getting three callers. The small blind completes.

Question: Call or fold?

 Answer: Call. You are getting 9-to-1 with mid suited connectors, and your call closes the action. Pay the extra t60 and see the flop. (There are six players and t720 in the pot.)

Flop: A♣8♥7♥

Action: The small blind checks.

Question: Check or bet?

 Answer: Check. While you do have an open-ended straight draw, your odds of winning the pot immediately are too little given the pre-flop raise, number of opponents, and the presence of an ace. Furthermore, if you are called and make a straight with the J♥ or 6♥, you may still lose to a heart flush. So check and hope for a free card.

Action: You check, the initial limper bets t145. The player to his left raises to t300 and everyone else folds.

Question: What is your move?

 Answer: Fold. Your odds of winning the pot immediately with a reraise are minuscule given this action, and the initial limper may still reraise so a call is out as well. Leave the hand.

Hands Where You Aggress Pre-flop, then Miss the Flop

 With a missed speculative hand, tend to check/fold every street. This is because you will usually have multiple opponents with a trash hand, facing a small pot.

 If, however, you were the pre-flop aggressor with a steal or premium hand, tend to make a bet of one-half to two-thirds the pot against few opponents all showing weakness (by checking at least once), and fold to a prior bet or raise to your bet. An example of this play is given in the pre-flop ace-king section.

Marginal Hands

If you are the big blind with

and the flop comes

or you limp with

and the flop comes

you have a marginal hand. It is probably best now, particularly if the field is small, but will often be beat by the river. If it's your action and no one has put chips in the pot, tend to bet around half the pot, hoping to take it immediately. If someone fires before you, or anyone plays back to your bet, abandon the hand.

There is a general principle guiding play of hands such as top pair, weak kicker. If the following criteria are met, tend to leave the hand:

1.   The pot is small

2.   Your hand is marginal

3.   You are not the aggressor

Leaving the pot when the above conditions hold is good general poker advice, and it is particularly applicable in low-blind tournament play.

Hand 1-20

Blinds: t20-t40, 9 players

Your hand: You (t1,940) have 9♠8♣ in the small blind.
Action to you: MP1 (t1,720) and the button (t1,940) limp.

Question: Fold or complete?

    Answer: Complete for t20. In general, if your hand has any showdown potential (suitedness, connectedness, or high card strength), put in the extra half-bet from the small blind if there are limpers and the blinds are low.

Action: You call and the big blind checks. (There are four players and t160 in the pot.)

Flop: 9♦4♣2♥

Question: Check or bet?

    Answer: Bet t100. You have top pair, so some type of bet is in order. But check-raising requires you to commit many more chips, and you are not looking to invest many chips this early with a hand likely to be best, but with little potential to improve if not.

Action: You bet t100. The big blind folds and both limpers call. (There are three players and t360 in the pot.)

Turn: 5♥

Question: Check or bet?

    Answer: Check. There were no likely draws at the flop, and while loose opponents could well be calling with a lower pair or even ace-high, it is not worth committing more chips to find out. Check, and hope you get a free river.

Action: You check, as does the first limper. The second limper bets t40.

Question: What is your move?

    Answer: Call. This bet could mean anything from a player milking a monster (a low set, in particular) to a weak bluff attempt. Getting 10-to-1 pot odds with top pair, however, you must at least call for another t40.

Action: You call, as does the first limper. (There are three players and t400 in the pot.)

River: J♣
Action: You check. MP1 checks. The button bets t67.[3]

Question: Fold or call?
Answer: Call. You could be up against a wide range of hands, but for a small bet offering better than 5-to-1, you should call with second pair.

Hand 1-21

Blinds: t30-t60, 10 players

Your hand: You (t1,960) have A♠8♣ in the big blind.
Action to you: All fold to the cut-off (t2,000), who calls, as do the button (t1,850) and the small blind (t2,400). You check. (There are four players and t240 in the pot.)

Flop: A♦6♥2♠
Action: The small blind checks.

Question: What is your move?
Answer: Bet around half the pot. It is very likely you have the best hand, and there is little for other players to call with. If you are raised, or called and do not improve, leave the hand. Do not get pot-committed in a small pot early in the tournament with a decent top pair hand. It is not strong

---

[3] The t67 is not a misprint. Players sometimes bet funny amounts.

enough. Indeed, refusing to walk away from a weak top pair hand is how many players bust out in ninth or tenth place. Avoid this trap. (However, since your top pair is specifically aces, it might be better to check-call or check-raise.)

Our next hand involves a simple psychological concept that is useful in any no-limit context.

Hand 1-22

Blinds: t20-t40, 10 players

Your hand: You (t1,940) have Q♠Q♦ as MP2.
Action to you: UTG (t2,000) raises to t120. The next two players fold. MP1 (t1,820) calls.

Question: What is your move?
 Answer: Raise to t450. With two opponents and an excellent, yet vulnerable, starting hand, you need to make a large raise. Winning the t300 pot immediately is a fine result, and if not, you want to limit the field to at most 1 to 2 opponents whom you have forced to make unprofitable calls.

Action: You raise to t450. All fold back to the initial raiser, who calls, as does MP1. (There are three players and t1,410 in the pot.)

Flop: K♠K♣9♥
Action: UTG bets t600. MP1 folds.

Question: What is your play?
 Answer: Raise all-in. You very likely have the best hand. If your opponent actually had a king, he would almost certainly check since you were the pre-flop aggressor and even beginners tend to slow-play in these situations. Why would

he make a big bet with flopped trips on a board with no obvious draws, against the pre-flop aggressor? In addition, the pot is a huge t2,000, and your reraise makes you the aggressor.

The above analysis is useful in many situations:

> If you are the pre-flop aggressor and an opponent bets out unexpectedly at the flop, then he is very unlikely to have a monster hand.[4]

With a good hand, he might be betting for value or to protect his hand. But with a monster and the reasonable expectation you will bet, the vast majority of players will slow-play by checking to you in this situation. Note that if there were still players behind you when the t600 bet was made, you would probably have to fold since one of those active players might be sitting on a king, or other strong hand, even if the initial bettor is on a stone bluff.

Hand 1-23

Blinds: t20-t40, 9 players

Your hand: You (t1,960) have A♦3♦ on the button.
Action to you: The first two players (t2,000 each) limp. You call with your suited ace in position. The small blind completes and the big blind checks. (There are five players and t200 in the pot.)

---

[4] An exception might be if he has read this book and thinks you have also read it. Against a smart player like this, a fold might be in order.

Flop: A♠9♥5♣

Action: The blinds check. The first limper bets t125. The second limper folds.

Question: Fold, call, or raise?

Answer: Fold. The pot is small, and if the bettor has an ace, you will lose a kicker battle. Betting out would have been reasonable, but here someone has already bet. The pot is not large, you are not the aggressor, and your hand is marginal. Leave the hand and don't look back.

Low-Blind Play: Summary

Play a cautious, tight-aggressive game during low-blind play. Before the flop, select only those hands you recognize as clearly equitable. If you are unsure whether to play a hand, fold as a default. But those hands you do play, proceed aggressively. When you enter a pot, it should usually be done with a raise, unless it is a speculative hand. Post-flop, again play aggressively — value-betting your good hands and tending to raise or fold otherwise (unless you are on a draw in a multiway pot and the bet comes from your right).

While these recommendations may seem on the cautious side, mistakenly getting involved in a large pot is a huge mistake during low-blind play. Stick to this level of tightness, while maintaining an aggressive style, and you will be fine. The greater your experience at no-limit, the more hands you may elect to play. This is particularly true if you are confident in your post-flop skills such as analyzing the texture of the flop, and knowing when you are beat in marginal situations.

But regardless, you always need a greater edge than if you were playing cash poker, since plays with positive chip expectation may still lower you equity in the tournament environment. Sticking only to the hands discussed above is admittedly a tight approach, but it will keep you safe from early bust-outs, while still involving you in the most profitable of hands.

Now it is time for mid-blind play. You will need to stay more active to keep ahead of the escalating blinds.

Part Two

Mid-Blind Play

Mid-Blind Play

Introduction

In our discussion of low-blind play, we emphasized that a looser style could be utilized by more advanced no-limit players. Indeed, the author knows empirically of winning loose-aggressive sit 'n go players (at the higher stakes, in particular), who exploit tight game conditions by loosening up. They then compensate for this naturally tougher-to-play style with shrewd post-flop play.

This same flexibility applies to mid-blind play. While most players should stick to the recommendations here, experienced shallower-stacked no-limit cash players and/or multi-table tournament players may expand the hands they play beyond the recommendations to follow. But now our default strategy naturally involves entering more pots and playing a more aggressive game.

In particular, while you should play the same categories of hands as during low-blind play, you must change gears to a more aggressive and pro-active style. We will begin ... through aggressive play.

Hands to Play
During Mid Blinds

Premium Hands

Premium hands are played similarly to the lower blinds. There tend to be fewer opponents contesting a pot as the blinds rise, however, and so you will often raise less, relative to the blinds. But if the big blind is a loose caller, bet a larger amount for value.

For instance, if you have

in the cut-off during t50-t100 blinds, a good default raise is t250. But if you know the big blind is a very loose caller, make a larger raise of t300 to t400.

If you get all the chips in the center before the flop, excellent. If everyone folds, winning immediately is always acceptable since the blinds are higher. If your pre-flop raise gets one or more callers, tend to get all your chips in on the flop if it is favorable (i.e., your high cards hit or all undercards come to your high pair). If the flop is uncooperative, you must use your judgment. With few opponents and everyone showing weakness, you should often take a stab at the pot.

Hand 2-1

Blinds: t50-t100, 9 players

Your hand: You (t2,000) have A♠A♣ on the button. Both blinds (t2,100 and t1,250) are tight-aggressive.

Action to you: Everyone folds to you.

Question: Call or raise, and if you raise, how much?
   Answer: Raise to t225. You want value for you hand, and calling is too weak. A small raise is your best option. The shorter-stacked TAG big blind may even reraise this weak-looking steal attempt with a decent hand. (However, against a weak-tight player a flat call can be the better play.)

Hand 2-2

Blinds: t100-t200, 8 players

Your hand: You (t1,500) have A♠K♣ on the button. The big blind (t2,900) is loose-passive.
Action to you: The loose-passive MP2 (t2,400) limps. Everyone else folds.

Question: Do you call, raise all-in, or raise a lesser amount?
   Answer: Push all-in now. There is t500 on the table, a full third of your stack, and you are happy to take it immediately with your ace-high hand. Furthermore, any lesser raise will pot-commit you, forcing you into a difficult decision post-flop if you are called and miss your hand. Take the money on the table, or force the limper or loose, big-stacked big blind to gamble for the full t1,500 before seeing the flop.

Make the same play here with any other premium hand vulnerable to many flops yet likely to be best now, such as jacks or tens.

Hand 2-3

Blinds: t50-t100, 10 players

Your hand: You (t1,700) have K♠K♣ as MP1.
Action to you: Everyone folds.

Question: What is your move?
> **Answer:** Raise to t250. While you don't mind action, you must raise to prevent a chain of callers, and the exact amount depends on your table — t200 will often win the pot immediately against a field of rocks, whereas t350 may yield several callers against many loose-passive opponents. t250 is a solid number because it is enough to limit the field while still allowing an aggressive opponent to reraise.

Action: Everyone folds to the tightish big blind (t1,800) who calls. (There are two players and t550 in the pot.)

Flop: 6♣4♣2♠
Action: He checks.

Question: What is your play?
> **Answer:** Bet t400. Your hand is almost certainly best. So win the pot right now or charge him steeply for a flush or other draw.

Action: He reraises to t1,600, putting you all-in.

Question: Fold or call?

> **Answer:** Call. He most likely has a hand such as A♣J♣ or a lower overpair. With cards that make two pair or a made straight, he wouldn't have called your pre-flop raise. While a made set is possible, you cannot always fear the worst, and in addition, most players would not play a hand this strong so aggressively at the flop against an opponent who is already doing the betting. Remember, most players will slow-play monster hands. With a high overpair in heads-up mid-blind play, you need very compelling evidence you are beat to fold, and a big bet at this ragged board does not qualify.

Action: You call, and he shows 8♠8♣. Your kings hold up to win the pot.

Hand 2-4

Blinds: t50-t100, 8 players

Your hand: You (t1,650) have Q♠Q♣ in the cutoff.
Action to you: Everyone folds.

Question: What is your move?

> **Answer:** Raise to t300. Winning immediately with queens is fine, and you should make an opponent with a king or ace pay for the opportunity to outdraw you.

Action: The small blind (t1,400) calls and the big blind folds. (There are two players and t650 in the pot.)

Flop: K♦6♥2♠
Action: Your opponent checks.

Question: Check or bet?
Answer: Bet t300. This bet is enough to win the pot if your opponent does not have a king, yet you are not pot-committed if he plays back.

Action: You bet t300 and he check-raises to t800.

Question: Do you fold, call, or reraise?
Answer: Fold. You showed strength before and after the flop, and yet your opponent came back over top on a board with no obvious draws for most of his chips. It is very likely he has a king (ace-king if tight, any high king or king-x suited if loose), and you cannot risk your remaining chips to find out. Fold your queens.

Speculative Hands

Speculative hands should be played sparingly during mid-blind play. This is because with higher blinds, limping costs a non-negligible portion of your stack, and an opponent later to act may elect to raise, making you walk away from your sizeable investment. So conditions need to be optimal.

In particular, you should be late to act, with several limpers, ideally holding a low-mid pocket pair. If you have reason to believe a raise is more likely than normal from someone to act after you, do not limp. In addition, the smaller your stack, the less often you should limp with a speculative hand. There are two reasons for this.

1. If you are shorter-stacked, you will often want to play, but with a raise — usually all-in — rather than merely calling. (See the section "Multiple High-Blind Limpers" starting on page 102 in "Part Two: Mid-Blind Play" for more on this topic.)

2. The greater your stack, the less the value of the chips you are risking. This is because of declining chip value, as discussed earlier. Therefore limping with a small stack requires a greater equity investment (aka costs more) than limping with a bigger stack.

Let us elaborate on this last point with an example: Suppose you are playing a $109 sit 'n go and the blinds are t100-t200. How much more does it cost (in dollars) for a player with t1,000 (in chips) to limp than a player with t5,000 (in chips)?

Answer: First, let us make a rough estimate of what these numbers should be. Your t200 chip investment is 1 percent of the t20,000 total chips in play, and these t20,000 in chips are for a total prize pool of $1,000. So a reasonable first guess is that a t200 chip limp represents (1 percent)($1,000) = $10.

But as we have stated, chips decline in value the more one has. So we turn to the Independent Chip Model, an algorithm to convert chip stacks into equities. While chip counts are not the only criteria for determining equity (skill, in particular, is a crucial factor), ICM remains a valuable tool to account for declining chip worth when assessing equity.

We plug in sample stacks for the remaining opponents and use the Independent Chip Model to estimate the value of t200 in chips for the t1,000 stack player versus his t5,000 stack counterpart.

t1,000 chip stack: $57 equity
t800 chip stack: $46 equity

$57 - $46 = $11 for t200 in chips

t5,000 chip stack: $229 equity
t4,800 chip stack: $222 equity

$229 - $222 = $7 for t200 in chips

So it is as if you are playing a cash game and one player limps for $7 while you must pay $11 to do the same. Clearly you would be less inclined to play when limping costs an extra $4. Regardless of the exact dollar amounts, realize that mid and high-blind limping is more costly with a small stack, and therefore you should do it rarely.[5]

Hand 2-5

Blinds: t50-t100, 8 players

Your hand: You (t1,480) are the small blind with 3♠3♣.

Action to you: The loose-aggressive chip leader (t3,600) limps from UTG+1. Everyone else folds to the button (t2,200) who calls.

Question: Fold, Call, or Raise?

> **Answer:** Call. Folding is out of the question. Raising all-in is reasonable. The t350 on the table represents nearly 25 percent of your stack, and no one has shown strength. But calling allows you to see a flop cheaply with the potential to win a great number of chips in a pot with three others, including the big-stacked limping LAG, from whom you are likely to win many chips if you flop a set.

Hand 2-6

Blinds: t50-t100, 8 players

---

[5] Another way to think about this is that the penalty to you for losing, assuming you have the small stack, is greater than the penalty would be for the large stack.

Your hand: You (t2,450) have T♠9♠ in the big blind. The cutoff (t3,300) is loose-aggressive.

Action to you: All fold to the cutoff who min-raises to t200. The button folds and the small blind calls.

Question: What is your move?

> **Answer:** Call. The implied odds with high suited connectors against a maniac are too good to pass up, particularly with immediate pot odds of 5-to-1 and well over 20BB left in your stack. (There are three players and t600 in the pot.)

Flop: 9♣6♦3♥

Action: The small blind checks.

Question: Check or bet?

> **Answer:** Bet around t400. You have a very vulnerable hand and you cannot risk your loose opponent checking behind if you check. So make a solid bet to protect your hand.

Action: You bet t400. The limper calls and the small blind folds. (There are two players and t1,400 in the pot.)

Turn: A♣

Question: Check or bet?

> **Answer:** Check. Two bad things have happened. First, your LAG opponent may well have you beat. He is aggressive, raised before the flop, and then merely called a big bet on the flop with a raggedy board. The pre-flop and flop betting rounds indicate he has a pocket pair above nines, or possibly a set of sixes. And any holding that did not have you beat at the turn, such as A♥K♥, would almost have to improve with the turn ace.

If the turn had come another blank, say the 2♠, you might take the risk and attack this big pot. But with an ace on board, you are probably better off check/folding except to a small bet.

Action: You and your opponent both check.

River: J♠

Question: Check or bet?
> **Answer:** Bet t200. If you check, he will almost certainly bet, either for value or as a bluff. You will have to call any reasonable bet with mid pair, and so it is probably better to bet yourself. You may well be called with an inferior hand, such as a low pocket pair. Furthermore, with two overcards to the board, you can make a fairly safe laydown to a raise of any size.

Hand 2-7

Blinds: t50-t100, 9 players

Your hand: You (t2,220) have J♠T♠ in the small blind.
Action to you: A loose-passive player (t2,000) limps from middle position. Everyone else folds.

Question: Fold or call?
> **Answer:** Call. You are getting a discount on a quality speculative hand, and it is worth another t50 to see the flop.

Action: You call and the big blind checks. (There are three players and t300 in the pot.)

Flop: J♣T♦2♥

Question: Check or bet?

Answer: Bet t200. You do not want to give a free card, nor do you want to shut out the big blind by check-raising the likely bettor — the limper. So lead out. If everyone folds, that's fine. If you get raised, push all-in with your top two pair. And if your bet gets smooth-called, you will want to make a larger bet at the turn.

Action: You bet t200. The big blind folds and the limper calls. (There are two players and t700 in the pot.)

Turn: A♥

Question: Check or bet?

Answer: Bet t400. This is a bad card. If your opponent was staying in with any pair and an ace kicker, he now has a better two pair. King-queen would also be consistent with his pre-flop and flop calls, and is now a straight. He could also be holding onto two hearts. But heads-up your hand is probably best, and since you would have to call a bet were one made, bet out yourself.

Action: You bet t400 and he calls. (There are two players and t1,500 in the pot.)

River: 3♣

Question: Check or bet?

Answer: Bet another t400. Since you would again have to call a reasonable bet, it is best to make it yourself. This bet gives you value if you have the best hand (which is likely). Furthermore, it has a defensive aspect. You showed considerable strength on the flop and turn, and it will be very difficult for an opponent, particularly a passive one, to go over you with a worse hand. If he does come over the top, lay the hand down and save your remaining t1,100.

Action: You bet t400. He calls, showing K♥T♣. Your two pair take the pot.

The above two examples are anomolies, of course — the majority of the time your speculative hand will miss. When it does, since you will tend to be up against multiple opponents with these hands, simply throw your hand away.

Hand 2-8

Blinds: t50-t100, 9 players

Your hand: You (t2,400) have 2♠2♣ on the button.
Action to you: Three of the first seven players limp, including the TAG under-the-gun. The blinds are passive.

Question: Fold, call, or raise?
   Answer: Call. Raising a pot-sized amount to win immediately or take the hand heads-up to the flop with a lot of dead money would usually be a reasonable alternative, but a tight-aggressive early limper is often trapping. With your large stack and speculative hand, simply call.

Action: You call and both blinds elect to see the flop for t100. (There are six players and t600 in the pot.)

Flop: T♦4♦3♣
Action: Everyone checks to you.

Question: Check or bet?

    Answer: Check. With five opponents and a missed speculative hand, do not put another penny into the pot unless you improve for free.

Blind-Stealing Hands

    Late position steal hands are now your bread and butter. These are hands where you make an open-raise with the intention of winning the now-sizeable blinds before the flop. You also want cards that afford a reasonable chance of winning after the flop if called.

    When evaluating whether to play a blind-stealing hand, ask yourself the following three questions:

1.   **How late is your position?** If you are in the small blind and all have folded to you, there is only one remaining player to contend with. By contrast, steal-raising as MP1 leaves 6 active opponents who may call or reraise.

2.   **How strong is your hand?** You must evaluate your potential to connect with the flop. For instance,

requires you to hit one card, the king, and even then you have the worst kicker possible. By contrast, hands such as

and

have straight, flush, top pair with good kicker, or even just double-overcard potential.

3. **How likely are your remaining opponents to fold to your raise?** Note that this question is independent of your hand strength, since your opponents do not know your hand when they react to your bet. Is the big blind a big-stacked loose-aggressive player who will call or raise with any two, or is he a timid player who would only defend his blind with a monster hand? The tighter and more passive the remaining opponents (and big blind in particular), the more likely you should be to steal.

Your stack size is also crucial. With under 10 big blinds, a blind-stealing raise is essentially pot-committing, and therefore you should tend to push all-in when you do steal.

For example, suppose you have a stack of 9BB and steal-raise to 3BB. If you are called, then your stack will be 6BB and you will be playing a pot worth 6.5BB or higher. If you are reraised all-in, you will be getting better than 2-to-1 odds for a call. This is a terrible situation. You are forced to surrender your sizeable chip investment or commit the remainder of your small stack to the pot. Therefore, you should make the initial all-in raise yourself to maximize your chances of winning the pot.

> With a stack fewer than 10BB, if you intend to blind-steal, push all-in rather than make a smaller raise.

Meanwhile, with a larger stack of 15 to 20 (or more) big blinds, your winning chances do not significantly diminish if you are forced to abandon the hand to a re-steal or unfavorable flop. So you should not hesitate to make a standard blind-stealing raise.

Most difficult to play is the moderate stack, perhaps 9 to 14 big blinds in chips. You usually do not want to risk an entire stack this large on an all-in steal, yet if you are forced to abandon your smaller raise in the face of unfavorable action, this represents a damaging blow to your stack.

For instance, if the blinds are t50-t100 and you (t1,150) raise to t300, folding to an unfavorable flop or pre-flop reraise leaves you with a comparatively meager t850. So you want the three blind-stealing conditions listed above — your hand, your position, and your opponents likelihood to fold — to be favorable.

Now let us suppose you have decided to blind-steal, and consider some possible results. If everyone folds, this is ideal as you have won the blinds without a fight. If you are reraised, you will usually have to let a non-premium hand go and move on.

It is when you are merely called that you will face more difficult decisions in post-flop play. There are three basic guiding principles:

1. If you hit the flop solidly, bet for value relentlessly. For instance, if you raise with K♦J♣ and the flop comes king high, bet the flop and keep on betting.

2.   If you miss the flop entirely, your default should be to make a continuation bet of around one-half to one-third the pot. This is because you must take a stab at the pot after your pre-flop show of strength, but you must also avoid risking any more than necessary. A half pot-sized bet is a good default for this purpose. If your opponent bets first or reraises, leave the hand.

3.   If you hit a smaller piece of the flop, such as mid pair, low pair, or a straight or flush draw, tend to bet or raise the flop, but avoid committing more chips if you do not win the pot at the flop and do not improve.

Let us look at some concrete examples of blind-stealing hands, and the post-flop play that occurs should you be called.

Hand 2–9

Blinds: t50-t100, 9 players

Your hand: You (t1,800) have T♠T♥ as MP3.
Action to you: Everyone folds.

Question: What is your move?
   Answer: Raise to t300. You have an excellent hand in mid-late position. Come in for a standard raise.

Action: You raise to t300 and are called only by the big blind (t2,100). (There are two players and t650 in the pot.)

Flop: 9♦8♣3♠
Action: He checks.

Question: Check or bet?

> **Answer:** Bet t500. Your overpair is almost certainly best, but will be severely devalued if an overcard hits. Make a pot-sized bet to protect your hand.

Hand 2-10

Blinds: t50-t100, 9 players

Your hand: You (t1,350) have K♠J♠ in the cutoff seat. Both blinds (t1,840 and t2,200) are tight-aggressive.

Action to you: Everyone folds.

Question: What is your move?

> **Answer:** Raise to t250. Despite being in the 10 to 14BB moderate zone, you have a solid hand in late position, so come in with a raise of standard 2 to 3 big blinds.

Action: Your raise to t250. The button folds. The tight small blind (t1,900) calls and the big blind folds. (There are two players and t600 in the pot.)

Flop: A♠Q♥2♥

Action: He checks.

Question: What is your move?

> **Answer:** Check. Normally you would make a continuation bet of around t300 or t350 here. But you should be concerned that a TAG smooth-called your raise from the small blind, and if he does come over the top of your bet (as an aggressive player is more likely to do), you must fold, leaving yourself well under 10BB (in chips). Check now but bet the next card if you make your straight or he shows weakness by checking again.

Action: You check.

Turn: 8♦
Action: He checks.

Question: Check or bet?
    Answer: Usually bet about t350. He may have a mid pocket pair and assume you have hit one of the overcards. Or he may have ace-queen and be trapping. Regardless, he has shown too much weakness for you not to take one stab at winning this pot. If he raises, you can make a safe laydown, and you also have four straight outs in case of a smooth-call.

Hand 2-11

Blinds: t100-t200, 8 players

Your hand: You (t1,750) have A♠2♣ on the button.
Action to you: Everyone folds.

Question: What is your play?
    Answer: Raise all-in. An ace on the button is usually good enough to blind-steal, and with under 10BB (in chips), you should often raise all-in rather than make a smaller, yet still pot-committing bet. An exception to this steal attempt occurs when your opponents play particularly poorly, and you feel that you will have better opportunities to exploit their weak play in future hands by declining this slightly profitable blind-steal.

Hand 2-12

Blinds: t50-t100, 9 players

Your hand: You (t2,100) have A♥5♥ on the button.
Action to you: Everyone folds.

Question: What is your move?
 Answer: Raise to t250 with your suited ace in position.

Action: Your raise to t250 and are called by the loose small blind (t2,800). The big blind folds. (There are two players and t600 in the pot.)

Flop: K♥5♣3♠
Action: He min-bets t100.

Question: Fold, call, or raise?
 Answer: Raise to t400. Mid pair is strong heads-up, and even if you are behind, your pair and backdoor flush draw (over 6 outs total) will improve by the river 25 percent of the time. If you are reraised, lay the hand down. But that is unlikely. You are showing tremendous strength through your pre-flop raise and flop raise. If he has a hand strong enough to come back over the top — such as top pair, good kicker, or a set — he probably would have checked the flop, knowing that you would likely bet as the pre-flop aggressor, thereby allowing him to check-raise.

Hand 2-13

Blinds: t50-t100, 9 players

Your hand: You (t2,300) have Q♠J♠ on the button. The blinds are tight-passive.
Action to you: MP1 raises to t300, and all else fold to you.

Question: Fold, call, or raise?

   Answer: Fold. With high suited connectors on the button, you would gladly blind-steal were the pot unopened. But MP1 has already made a solid raise, so you cannot hope to pick up the blinds uncontested. Your hand is not strong enough to reraise, and you should usually avoid smooth-calling pre-flop raises.

Hand 2-14

Blinds: t100-t200, 6 players

Your hand: You (t3,100) have J♠T♠ in the small blind. The big blind (t900) is loose.

Action to you: Everyone folds.

Question: What is your move?

   Answer: Raise all-in. Your jack-ten suited is a considerably above average hand, certainly worth a steal attempt. Normally you should not push all-in with your 15+BB stack, but in this case, your one opponent has a stack of t900 after posting. Therefore your bet is effectively t1,100 (as you must match his blind as well), since anything you bet beyond this enters a sidepot that you automatically win.

   This principle is discussed more in the section, "Adjusting to Different Stack Sizes: Mid Blind" starting on page 123 in "Part Two: Mid-Blind Play."

Hand 2-15

Blinds: t50-t100, 8 players

Your hand: You (t2,000) have K♦Q♠ in the hijack position.
Action to you: Everyone folds.

Question: What is your move?
    Answer: Make a standard blind-stealing raise to t300.

Action: All fold to the tight big blind, who calls the extra t200.
There are two players and t650 in the pot.

Flop: A♥9♦2♠
Action: The big blind checks.

Question: Check or bet?
    Answer: Bet t300. *You must always ask yourself what you
are trying to accomplish by betting.* This lower bet is
sufficient to tell you whether he has the ace, and it figures to
win the pot for you if he does not. Since there are no flush or
straight draws, your tight opponent will not stick around
without the ace after you have shown strength pre-flop and
made a follow-up bet when the ace hits. In particular, he will
probably discard a hand such as 7♣7♥. If your bet does get
called or raised, you are done putting money in the pot, and
may still walk away with plenty of chips to remain in
contention. If instead you make a pot-sized bet, you take the
pot equally if he has no ace, but you are throwing away the
extra money if he comes back over top of you.

> Never bet more than is necessary to bluff
> down a pot you will not win at showdown.

Hand 2-16

Blinds: t100-t200, 9 players

Your hand: You (t3,100) have K♣J♠ on the button. The big blind (t2,400) is loose-passive.

Action to you: Everyone folds.

Question: What is your play?
    Answer: Raise to t500. You have two face cards on the button and this warrants a raise.

Action: You raise to t500. The small blind folds. The big blind reraises all-in.

Question: Call or fold?
    Answer: Fold. The pot is t2,400 (his reraise) + t300 (the blinds) + t500 (your bet) = t3,200, and it costs you t1,900 to call. Despite getting well over 3-to-2, you should fold. This call will be for most of your stack and a passive player making an uncharacteristically aggressive move indicates genuine strength. Thus his range of hands will be more than 60 percent against you. Lay this one down and move on.

Hand 2-17

Blinds: t50-t100, 9 players

Your hand: You (t2,500) have Q♦9♠ on the button.

Action to you: Six folds, leaving only you and the tight-passive blinds (t1,900 and t2,100).

Question: What is your move?
    Answer: Raise to t250. When it is folded to you on the button, you should steal raise liberally against tight-passive blinds (the big blind being of particular importance). Here you have an above average hand and an above average stack, so make a standard raise of 2½ or 3 big blinds.

Hand 2-18

Blinds: t50-t100, 9 players

Your hand: You (t2,500) have Q♦9♠ in the cut-off. The big blind is loose-aggressive (t2,100).
Action to you: Everyone folds.

Question: What is your move?
> **Answer:** Fold. Unlike the last hand, you should discard your queen-nine offsuit here. You have one more active opponent who will have position after the flop should he call, but more importantly, the combination of a loose-aggressive big blind and your marginal holding cement this into a fold. Wait for a better opportunity to blind-steal.

Hand 2-19

Blinds: t50-t100, 7 players

Your hand: You (t1,600) have 8♠8♣ in the cut-off.
Action to you: Everyone folds.

Question: Fold, call, or raise?
> **Answer:** Raise to t300. You have a significantly above-average hand in late position during mid-blind play. Attack the blinds with a solid raise of 3 or 4BB.

Action: You raise to t300. The button (t1,900) calls. The small blind folds. The big blind (t1,400) calls. (There are three players and t950 in the pot.)

Flop: K♦8♦3♦
Action: The big blind checks.

Question: What is your move?

    Answer: Push all-in. Two observations are key in your decision to push:

1.   You are very likely to have the best hand, and even if someone did flop the flush, you will improve to a winning full house over one-third of the time. However, if you allow another card, your hand will be devalued to mere bluff-catching status should a fourth diamond fall.

2.   The pot currently has t950, nearly three-fourths of your remaining stack.

The combination of a large pot and an excellent, yet supremely vulnerable, made hand make this a pushing situation.

Hand 2-20

Blinds: t100-t200, 7 players

Your hand: You (t1,600) have 8♠8♣ in the cut-off.
Action to you: Everyone folds to you.

Question: Fold, call, or raise?

    Answer: Raise all-in. This hand is identical to the last one except now your stack is 8BB rather than 16BB. Your position and hand strength still dictate a blind-steal, but with a short stack, raise all-in rather than make a smaller bet.

Hand 2-21

Blinds: t50-t100, 10 players

Action to you: You (t1,890) are UTG with A♠Q♣.

Question: Fold, call, or raise?

    Answer: Fold. Besides short-handed high-blind play, ace-queen offsuit should be folded from early position (unless you are on a short atack). There is little on the table, and anyone who calls your raise may outkick you with ace-king if the ace hits. Do not get involved.

Hand 2-22

Blinds: t50-t100, 8 players

Your hand: You (t1,900) have A♠Q♠ on the button. The blinds (t1,800 and t3,100) are loose-passive.

Action to you: Everyone folds to you.

Question: What is your move?

    Answer: Raise to t350. Pushing is probably wrong as you have nearly 20BB in chips. And while you normally should not blind-steal against calling stations, your hand is much too strong to fold. A larger raise to 3½ blinds will force your opponents to surrender the pot now, or pay too much with a worse hand out of position. An alternate option would be to flat-call the $100, thereby taking advantage of your strong hand and positional advantage while keeping the pot small. But you should only consider smooth-calling in situations like these if you have the post-flop skills to know when your top pair is beat, so that you will not go broke playing a small pot if one of the blinds connects solidly with the flop.

Action: The small blind folds, but the big blind calls for another t250. (There are two players and t750 in the pot.)

Flop: Q♥J♣2♠
Action: The blind checks.

Question: What is your move?

> **Answer:** Bet t450. You hit the flop solidly and your goal is to get value for your hand.

Action: You bet t450, and he calls. (There are two players and t1,650 in the pot.)

Turn: 8♥

Action: Your opponent bets t100.

Question: What do you do?

> **Answer:** Raise all-in. The pot is t1,750, and you have just over t1,000 left. With top pair, top kicker you cannot leave this hand. So bet the rest of your chips now, forcing your opponent to abandon this huge pot, or beat your heads-up monster hand at showdown.

Steals and Re-Steals

Distinguishing Steal Raises from Value Raises

Before discussing the crucial re-steal play of next section, we must learn how to classify a raise. When someone makes a raise during mid-blind play, his motive may be broken down into two components:

1. Desire to steal the blinds.

2. Wanting value on a superior holding.

If you act after the raiser, your job is to figure out whether his raise is primarily a blind-steal, or primarily a value raise. The two important criteria for deciding are bettor aggressiveness and bettor position. The more passive the bettor, the more likely he is raising with an actual hand. Similarly, the earlier he is to act, the more likely he has a strong hand.

The size of the bet relative to the bettor's stack and the blinds may also be significant. If the size of the raise is unexpected, this often indicates a strong hand. This is because most players sense they should behave trickily with their real hands and tricky implies different from normal.

For example, if a tight-passive player who never raises before the flop doubles the big blind from MP1, he almost certainly has a hand. Similarly, a tight-aggressive player who always pushes when short-stacked relative to the blinds, is liable to have a premium hand when only min-raising from late position with a short stack.

Exercise: Classify the following raises as value or steal. In each case, everyone has folded up to the raiser.

1. Blinds t50-t100: A passive player (t900) raises to t300 with five players left to act.

2. Blinds t100-t200: A tight-aggressive player (t3,500) raises to t550 on the button.

3. Blinds t50-t100: A very aggressive player (t1,500) raises to t300 from UTG. This opponent routinely blind-steals with raises of t300.

4. Blinds t200-t400: The loose-passive small blind (t1,750) pushes all-in on the big blind (t2,400).

Answers:

1. **Value raise.** An aggressive play from a normally-passive opponent indicates strength. His non-late position confirms this hypothesis.

2. **Steal.** A TAG raising to 2.5 to 3 big blinds from late position is almost always stealing.

3. **Value.** Any time an opponent raises from early position, you should assume he has a hand.

4. **Steal.** Anytime the blinds are big and all fold up to the small blind, who proceeds to move all-in, you should be thinking "Steal."

Note that this distinction is not black-and-white, and a raise may have both value and steal purposes. However, you still want to think about the bettor's primary reason for deciding to raise.

Doing so will allow you to aggress violently and intelligently with a play called ...

The Re-Steal (RS)

There are two types of steal-raises in tournament poker: the steal and the re-steal (RS). The steal raise is a late position raise to win the blinds. The re-steal is a late position reraise to win the blinds as well as the initial steal.

You should consider a re-steal when the following three criteria are met:

1. An earlier-to-act opponent makes a raise you classify as primarily steal. This steal classification increases the likelihood his hand will lack sufficient strength to call your re-steal.

2. You have reasonable showdown potential. Clearly you want a hand which does not figure to be a severe underdog should you be called.

3. The steal is large enough such that the pot represents a significant fraction of your current stack, yet not so large that a reraise on your part leaves your opponent pot-committed to call.

We will see the specifics of these criteria in the hand examples below.

The re-steal allows you to be the ultimate aggressor, representing great strength by committing most or all your chips after a player has already raised. Opponents will often fold even solid hands rather than risk their entire tournament life against an opponent showing such strength. Furthermore, nobody can play back at you once you have committed all your chips, and taking the pot without a fight represents a vast gain when you are winning both the blinds and the steal.

If your re-steal gets called by a premium hand, then your "steal" assessment was wrong. Distinguishing steal raises from value raises is not an exact science, but you should carefully review the hand afterward and see if there might have been a clue the initial raise was actually for value.

If you get called by a non-premium hand, then while this is still an undesirable result, at least your decent hand may be able to hold up to win a monster pot. You should, however, make sure your stack was big enough that the stealer could get away from his raise. Do not re-steal a pot-committed opponent.

It is entirely possible for an opponent to randomly call with any decent or average hand, particularly big stacks at lower buy-in sit 'n go's. If this is the case, and the cards do not come your way, then do not worry. Your aggressive play will pay off in the long run.

Whether to fold or place all your chips at risk on a big re-steal can be a difficult decision. We will analyze several of the crucial decision-making factors in the problems that follow.

Hand 2-23

Blinds: t100-t200, 4 players

Your hand: You (t1,700) are on the button with K♠J♣. The small blind (t4,500) and big blind (t5,800) have been inactive for several hands, as have you. The blinds will soon rise to t200-t400.

Action to you: The LAG chip leader (t8,000), first to act, makes a characteristic min-raise to t400.

Question: Do you fold, call, or reraise?

Answer: Re-steal all-in. There is t700 in the pot, over 40 percent of your stack. You have a decent hand with showdown potential, and the chip leader will often back away from a foiled steal attempt.

In addition, you need to gamble here. With the big blind at over 10 percent of your stack and just about to double, and the blinds hitting you constantly at 4-way play, you need to make a move. A situation like this one, when you have a decent hand and are the aggressor against opponents who have shown little strength, is the ideal place to risk your chips.

Hand 2-24

Blinds: t100-t200, 8 players

Your hand: You (t1,600) have Q♠9♠ in the big blind. The button (t2,400) is a loose player who routinely min-raises and has yet to be played back at.

Action to you: All fold to the button who min-raises to t400. The small blind folds.

Question: What is your move?
　　Answer: Push all-in. You have an above average hand, and it is clear the button will double with even marginal hands, so he will most likely fold rather than risk the majority of his stack (a call and loss would leave him with a mere t800). Meanwhile, there is already t700 on the table, nearly half your t1,600 stack. And if you get called, you should still win a reasonable portion of the time, as you will often be against small favorites such as A♥T♠ or 7♦7♥.

Hand 2-25

Blinds: t50-t100, 8 players

Your hand: You (t2,400) have K♠9♣ in the big blind.

Action to you: All fold to the aggressive button (t2,300) who raises to t300. The small blind folds.

Question: What is your move?

> **Answer:** Fold. You have a decent hand and are facing an almost certain steal raise. And yet, calling and raising are both problematic. If you call, you are playing a decent-sized pot (t650) out of position. Even if you hit the flop, you may be out-kicked if your opponent had a better-than-expected holding.
>
> Meanwhile, reraising all-in risks t2,300 to win t450, which is not a good enough return on your investment at a point when you are under no pressure to make a move. A smaller raise is more reasonable, but you will be pot-committing yourself if your opponent does not leave the hand, an unnecessary risk when you have well over 20 big blinds.

Hand 2-26

Blinds: t200-t400, 7 players

Your hand: You (t4,500) are the chip leader with K♠Q♠ on the button. The tight-aggressive blinds each have around t2,000.

Action to you: The loose-aggressive second chip leader (t3,800) raises to t1,000 from the hijack seat.

Question: What is your move?

> **Answer:** Push all-in. It is unlikely the LAG will want to risk his tournament life finding out what you have. The t1,600 you stand to win uncontested is huge, and will help give you a hammerlock over this table. And if he does call, you are only a significant underdog to a monster hand — AK, AQ, AA-QQ.

Hand 2-27

Blinds: t100-t200, 7 players

Your hand: You (t2,100) have A♠3♠ in the small blind. The button (t2,600) is tight-aggressive.

Action to you: All fold to the button whom you have previously seen make blind-stealing raises, who raises to t500.

Question: What is your move?

Answer: Reraise all-in. This is an obvious steal raise, and you have a decent hand. Tight-aggressive players hate being re-stealed when on a steal, and will fold unless pot-committed. If you do get called, you cannot be much worse than a 2-to-1 underdog with your suited ace unless your opponent has precisely pocket aces (e.g., against kings or ace-jack you are still nearly 2-to-1 to win the pot).

Hand 2-28

Blinds: t100-t200, 9 players

Your hand: You (t1,900) have A♠T♣ in the cutoff seat.

Action to you: Everyone folds to the loose-passive MP3 (t3,600) who raises to t750.

Question: What is your move?

Answer: Fold. First, when a loose-passive player enters in mid position for a raise, this usually indicates a strong hand. As important, your chances of winning before the flop are small as it is unlikely he will fold for another t1,150. There are also three active players left behind you. If you were about to be hit with higher blinds, gambling would be a solid option rather than getting blinded out. But as it is, lay this one down.

Hand 2-29

Blinds: t100-t200, 6 players

Your hand: You (t2,000) have 2♠2♣ in the big blind.
Action to you: Everyone folds to the small blind (t2,400) who raises to t600.

Question: What is your play?
    Answer: Reraise all-in. This is a situation where conditions are perfect for a re-steal. The raise is from the small blind, and so you should assume it is a steal raise. The t800 on the table represent a full 40 percent of your stack, a huge gain should he fold, and yet your stack is large enough that he is not pot committed to call a reraise. Lastly, your 2♠2♣ is about even money should he call with any non-pair hand such as A♥Q♥.

Hand 2-30

Blinds: t100-t200

Your hand: You (t1,400) are the button with Q♠9♠.
Action to you: All fold to the TAG cutoff (t3,000) who raises to t500.

Question: What is your move?
    Answer: Fold. You have a decent hand and are nearing short-stacked status, so a raise or re-steal is tempting. However, your TAG opponent will not fold for another t900. The pot odds would be too high, and the blow not crippling enough,

for even the most conservative player to make a laydown here.

Furthermore, your hand is likely to be an underdog to a pair or better high card hand. The aggressive instinct is a good one, but choose your spots carefully. Here your hand is non-premium, you are not desperate to make a move, and your opponent will call with a (often slightly) better hand most of the time. This is not the time to make a move.

Hand 2-31

Blinds: t50-t100, 9 players

Your hand: You (t2,000) have A♠T♠ on the button. The blinds (t1,400 and t1,900) are passive.

Action to you: The tight-passive UTG+1 (t1,800) raises to t300. Everyone else folds.

Question: What is your move?

    Answer: Fold. You have a quality hand, in late position, facing one raiser and passive blinds. But this is a value raise since the raiser is early to act and passive, and so you will often be called by a premium hand — a better ace or a pocket pair jacks or higher, in particular. In addition, you are risking all your chips to win the t450 on the table, which is under one-fourth of your stack. You have a decent chip position and are under no pressure to make a move. Save your chips for a better opportunity.

Now we explore the effects of a slight change in the pre-flop action.

Hand 2-32

Blinds: t50-t100, 9 players

Your hand: You (t2,000) have A♠T♠ on the button. The blinds (t1,400 and t1,900) are passive.

Action to you: Everyone folds to the aggressive hijack (t2,100) who raises to t400. The loose-passive cutoff (t2,900) calls.

Question: What is your move?

Answer: Reraise all-in. There are two key differences in this hand (compared to the last one):

1. Despite two opponents already active in the pot, much less strength has been shown. An aggressive player in mid-late position makes a standard steal raise, and is called by a big-stacked passive player. This is much less threatening than a single passive early position raiser since the hijack's motive is most likely a steal raise and by merely calling the passive cutoff did not show strength.

2. Related is the t950 on the table. This is nearly half your stack, and represents a huge gain in chips/equity if you win immediately. If the cutoff had folded, the t550 pot would represent a much smaller gain if you stole successfully.

With a solid hand such as ace-ten suited, you must take advantage of the favorable conditions you are being offered and make an aggressive play for all your chips.

There is a key re-stealing principle in this hand:

> You should be much more inclined to re-steal against a stealer and a caller(s) than against a single stealer.

This is because the pot grows enormously with each extra caller, yet no more strength has been shown. Sure, a tricky player might sometimes smooth-call a pre-flop raise with aces or kings. But in general, a second player who stays in the pot is showing weakness by not reraising, and you should attack this weakness when the pot is large and your hand has decent showdown potential.

Attacking Passivity and High-Percentage Raising

High-Blind Limpers (HBLs)

Any time you notice a player limping repeatedly after the low-blind stage has passed, label him High-Blind Limper (or "HBL") as a player note. You must notice this behavior more than once or see the player flip a non-premium holding at showdown after limping at mid-high blinds before you use this information. Otherwise you are vulnerable to aggressive players who limp hoping to reraise.

Once you have ascertained your opponent is a genuine HBL, be inclined to go over him with more hands than normal. Knowing that your opponent will limp at high blinds without a premium holding is valuable information. If you are short-stacked (under ten big blinds), you should often move all-in with a marginal hand such as

a low pocket pair, or mid suited connectors if you are late to act and no one else has voluntarily put chips in the pot.

Since there will be over one quarter of your stack on the table and nobody has shown strength, this is an excellent opportunity to make a move with any combination of a decent hand and position (to minimize the likelihood of an unexpected player calling with a monster). This important topic will be discussed in greater detail in "Part Three: High-Blind Play" starting on page 129. For now, here are some examples.

Hand 2-33

Blinds: t100-t200

Your hand: You (t1,300) have K♠9♠ in the big blind.

Action to you: All fold to the loose-passive button (t2,400) who calls. He has limped several times during t50-t100 and t100-t200. The small blind folds.

Question: What is your move?

    Answer: Push all-in. The pot is t500, nearly 40 percent of your t1,300 stack. (Remember that the blind sitting in front of you is a bet you have already been forced to make, so winning it back is just as good as winning any other chips.) The button appears to be a high-blind limper and has shown no real strength by limping and you have a reasonable hand. Exploit these ideal conditions with an all-in raise.

    Incidentally, you will find that the loose-passive playing style is strongly correlated with high-blind limping.

Hand 2-34

Blinds: t50-t100, 9 players

Your hand: You (t2,400) have A♠Q♠ in the hijack seat.

Action to you: A loose-passive opponent (t1,800) limps from MP1 and everyone else folds to you.

Question: What is your move?

   Answer: Raise to t350. Your hand is too strong to fold, but with only t250 on the table and a stack of t2,400, pushing risks too many chips for the potential reward. Also, while your opponent is loose, you do not know yet for sure he is an HBL. So make a standard pot-sized raise with your position and strong hand.

Action: You raise to t350. Everyone folds back to the limper who calls. (There are two players and t850 in the pot.)

Flop: 5♦4♥2♠
Action: He checks.

Question: Bet or check?

   Answer: Bet t450. With 6 overcard outs that are almost certainly good, a gut shot straight draw, as well as a backdoor flush draw, you are approximately 40 percent to improve if called. Your hand is probably best right now though, and with the aggression you showed before the flop, a bet of around half the pot is perfect. If he missed, he will likely fold. But should he raise, you probably should fold (against a likely mid high overpair; e.g. 7♥7♠).

Note that a pot-sized bet is overkill. You have shown strength and are making a reasonable bet after the flop. If he does not fold, it is unlikely he would for another few hundred in chips.

Hand 2-35

Blinds: t100-t200, 8 players

Your hand: You (t2,400) have A♣8♣ in the cutoff seat.
Action to you: A tight opponent (t1,800) limps from UTG+1. Everyone else folds to you.

Question: What is your move?

    Answer: Fold. A tight opponent limping early may be trapping. Reraising all-in risks too many chips in a marginal spot. And any call or smaller raise leaves you vulnerable to a reraise from one of the three remaining players, or more likely, the initial limper.

    Lastly, you are in no desperate need to make a move with well over 10BB. You are much more inclined to make a move with a shorter stack, whereas losing a big pot here will cripple you. Do not get involved.

Now let us modify this hand to a situation where aggression is justified.

Hand 2-36

Blinds: t100-t200, t25 ante, 8 players

Your hand: You (t1,800) have A♠8♠ in the cutoff seat.
Action to you: All fold to the HBL hijack (t2,400), who calls.

Question: What is your move?

    Answer: Raise all-in. You are much more inclined to make a move with your shorter stack and more chips on the table from the dead ante money. You are also facing an opponent who is much less likely to be trapping, and your logical raise to take the pot, an all-in, does not leave you vulnerable to a reraise as you have already committed all your chips. So push.

Multiple High-Blind Limpers

In an earlier section we considered a hand where the presence of a second active player in the pot contributed to your decision to re-steal before the flop. Likewise, the presence of an additional high-blind limper can be a crucial factor in your decision to steal the pot pre-flop with an aggressive play.

Here's an important principle concerning multiple high-blind limpers:

> While the first player to limp in a mid- high-blind hand could have a premium holding, subsequent callers are trapping only rarely.

Explanation: This is similar to the parallel concept for re-stealing against a blind-stealer and subsequent caller(s). It is conceivable that a player — even an observed HBL — who open-limps is doing so with a premium hand to induce a steal-raise from a weaker hand. (While such open-limping from a passive player is usually literal, weak players can find such deception "fun" if nothing else.)

But it is nearly impossible for the second caller to be trapping since he already has one limper and both blinds in the pot as victims to attack with a raise if he actually held a premium hand. Instead, subsequent limpers most likely observe that they have increasingly favorable odds for a call, and thus they will tend to limp with correspondingly weaker hands.

So whether there is one HBL or multiple HBLs in the pot, you still have about the same chances of being called by a legitimate hand if you make a sizeable raise. But with multiple HBLs, there is correspondingly more money to be won immediately with an aggressive play.

The following hands show how and when to exploit the Multiple HBL situation.

Hand 2-37

Blinds: t100-t200, 8 players

Your hand: You (t1,400) have T♠9♠ in the big blind. The blinds will increase to t200-t400 in one minute.

Action to you: Pre-flop: Two observed HBLs (t2,400 and t1,900) limp from early-mid position, and the tighter button (t3,000) calls. The small blind (t1,200) completes.

Question: Check or raise?

> **Answer:** Raise all-in. There is already t1,000 on the table, no opponent has shown particular strength, and you have a hand that plays relatively well in case of a call. Plus you must make a move soon to avoid getting blinded out. So push now.

> There are three possible outcomes when you shove in all your chips in this situation.

1. **Everyone folds.** This is not unlikely. The first limper is a confirmed HBL, and makes a standard loose-passive limp with little understanding of position or pot odds; he could easily like his hand at first, but not be willing to risk a damaging blow to his stack in the face of your apparent strength. Then the rest, who got caught up in the calling chain of increasingly good pot odds, fold behind. You add t1,000 to your t1,400 stack without even seeing the flop, a huge victory.

2. **One HBL calls, and the rest fold.** This will occur when the first HBL was indeed trapping or simply wants to gamble with a decent hand, or when HBL No. 1 folds, but a later player decides to gamble due to the superior pot odds — often an intuitive, rather than conscious, justification. In this case, you are gambling for your

entire stack at somewhere between even money or a 4-to-1 underdog (versus an underpair or overpair, respectively), but the pot is padded with t600 — nearly half of your t1,400 stack — in dead money.

In addition, mid suited connectors hold up well against even a premium hand, and entering the flop as a 3-to-2 underdog is a common worst-case scenario. For example, you are almost exactly 40 percent against ace-king offsuit. (For more on this, see "Appendix D: Pre-flop Hand Probabilities" on page 257.) Let us take the conservative estimate that if one HBL calls, you will be a 2-to-1 underdog. In this case, your cEV is -t133.

$$-t133 = \left(\frac{1}{3}\right)(t1,400 + t1,000) + \left(\frac{2}{3}\right)(-t1,400)$$

Your calling opponent may well even flip an underpair making you and him even heading into the flop, and consequently making your play very positive cEV with all the dead money.

3. **Multiple HBLs call.** While this is a terrible outcome, it is very unlikely. For it requires a player who is part of the limping chain to witness an all-in raise, a call of this raise, and then still decide to call himself. Anything is possible (particularly in the low-stakes games), but this is illogical for almost any holding and consequently rare.

The first case where everyone folds is obviously ideal, and should occur at least 30 percent of the time. If we assume that the strange multiple caller scenario occurs 10 percent of the time, and costs an average of around half your stack, then a single call happens the remaining 60 percent of the time and so your overall expectation for this raise is t150.

$$t150 = (.30)(t1,000) + (.60)(-t133) + (.10)(-t700)$$

With barely enough chips to last two orbits with the new blinds, you are looking for any good opportunity to make a move. This manifestly positive cEV play qualifies. Take advantage of the huge sum already on the table, your robust hand, and the extreme pre-flop passivity and push here.

Hand 2-38

Blinds: t100-t200, 8 players

Your hand: You (t3,800) have K♠Q♠ in the cutoff seat.
Action to you: Two loose players (t3,100 and t1,400) limp from middle position, and everyone else folds to you.

Question: What is your move?
    Answer: Raise to t750. With t700 on the table, nobody showing strength, and a strong hand, you cannot fold. Raising all-in is too heavy with a stack of t3,800. Calling is acceptable, but weak. So make a pot-sized raise. If you take the pot immediately, great. If you get called, your hand connects well with many flops. And if the initial limper or another big-stacked player comes over you for most of your stack, you can still safely abandon your hand, maintaining a healthy stack of t3,000.

Hand 2-39

Blinds: t100-t200, 8 players

Your hand: You (t1,700) have 2♠2♣ in the hijack seat.

Action to you: A tight-passive player (t2,600) limps from MP1, and the tight player (t2,350) to your right calls.

Question: What is your move?

   Answer: Raise all-in. You have a robust hand, nobody has shown real strength, and there is t700 sitting on the table (a sizeable fraction of your t1,700 chip stack). What might worry you is the tightness of the limpers. This is a legitimate concern, but you should push anyway. First, recall that the second limper almost cannot be trapping since he is later to act and already has the early limper and the blinds as active opponents.

   If the first limper were tight-aggressive, and you had strong reason to believe such an uncharacteristic play represented strength, this would change to a (close) laydown. But passive players, even tighter ones, are liable to high-blind limp with hands they want to play but would not call an all-in with. Exploit that fact with a push here, particularly since the t700 significantly improve your winning chances with a stack of only t1,700 and the blinds doubling next to t200-t400.

Hand 2-40

Blinds: t50-t100, 9 players

Your hand: You (t770) have Q♠4♣ in the big blind.

Action to you: An HBL (t3,100) limps from UTG+2, and is called by the cutoff (t3,900). Everyone else folds.

Question: What is your move?

   Answer: Check. If you raise all-in it is probable you will be called by one of the two limpers as each is big-stacked and your raise is not enough to threaten either's chip position. You need a decent hand to make an aggressive move at this pot, and a low off-suit queen does not qualify. Take the free flop instead, and plan to commit your chips at the flop if you hit any piece of it and post-flop action is favorable.

Hand 2-41

Blinds: t100-t200, 7 players

Your hand: You (t1,480) have K♠T♣ on the button.
Action to you: An HBL (t2,300) limps in early position, getting two loose callers (t1,800 and t2,600) in middle position.

Question: What is your move?
> **Answer:** Push all-in. There is t900, over 60 percent of your stack, just sitting on the table. No one has shown genuine strength. You have a reasonable hand. Push!
> Failing to take advantage of this ideal situation is a mistake. One of the limpers may decide to call with a low-mid pocket pair or two decent high cards, but that is a risk you should gladly take with a reasonable holding and 60 percent of your dwindling stack available for the immediate taking.

> Any time you have a reasonable holding and there is a chance to win a sizeable fraction of your stack immediately, strongly consider moving in if you believe there is a good chance everyone will fold.

Bluffing

While there are many examples of semi-bluffing in this book, there are considerably fewer of pure bluffing. You should usually refrain from betting with no hand and no draw purely in the hopes people will fold, particularly at the lower stakes. With that said, there are a few situations where a total bluff may be your best play.

One example is when you are the pre-flop aggressor, catch no piece of the flop, and your single opponent shows weakness by checking. Then you should usually still make a post-flop continuation bet as part of an aggressive strategy. (If you have two overcards to a raggedy flop, then even this bet is actually a semi-bluff as you have 6 outs to improve to a high pair.)

Another example occurs in mid-high-blind play when there is a small pot between a limper (usually the small blind) and yourself in the big blind. The flop comes with a pair and a low card, such as

Your opponent checks and you make a small bet, or if he is aggressive and bets small himself, you make a modest bluff-raise. If your opponent does not immediately leave the hand, you are done putting money in the pot.

Notice that there are only five cards your opponent could hold that connect with the board, and your bet/raise is often enough to make him concede right there as it is improbable he has hit the flop in any manner. However, do not try this play against a loose-passive low stakes player who might call a bet or raise with any two cards.

Hand 2-42

Blinds: t100-t200, 6 players

Your hand: You (t2,440) have T♥2♠ in the big blind.
Action to you: All fold to the passive small blind (t2,400), who
  calls. You check. (There are two players and t400 in the pot.)

Flop: A♠K♥3♦
Action: He checks.

Question: Check or bet?
  Answer: Min-bet t200. It is unlikely he caught any piece of
  this hand, and if your bet takes down the pot more often than
  one time in three, it is positive cEV. In fact, expect this bet to
  win immediately roughly half the time, making it distinctly
  profitable.

Hand 2-43

Blinds: t200-t400, t25 Ante, 4 players

Your hand: You (t6,800) have K♥6♥ in the small blind. The big
  blind (t5,100) is tight.
Action to you: Everyone folds.

Question: Call, fold, or raise?
  Answer: Call. The pot is a full t700 due to the antes, and it
  costs t200 to call. With these excellent pot odds and an
  above-average hand you cannot fold. Raising to t1,200 or
  pushing all-in are both reasonable plays, but when the
  effective stack sizes are well above 10BB and you have a
  reasonable hand for post-flop play, a simple complete is often
  your best play.

Action: You call, and the big blind checks. (There are two players
  and t900 in the pot.)

Flop: J♠J♣2♥

Question: Check or bet?

> **Answer:** Bet t500. Your opponent is statistically very unlikely to hold a jack here, and he would almost certainly have raised you pre-flop if he was holding a pocket pair. Meanwhile, your pre-flop call and flop bet show some strength, and your tight opponent may even lay down a deuce rather than invest more chips in this spot. If you get played back at, make an easy fold.

Lastly, sometimes you should bluff when you are against few opponents and everyone has shown overwhelming weakness. Consider the following hand:

Hand 2-44

Blinds: t25-t50, 8 players

Your hand: You (t1,500) have 6♦5♦ in the small blind. The button (t1,940) is tight-passive, and you have little read on the big blind (t1,320).

Action to you: All fold to the button, who calls. Getting 5-to-1 with a quality speculative hand, you call for another t25. The big blind checks. (There are three players and t150 in the pot.)

Flop: K♣J♣3♦

Question: Check or bet?

> **Answer:** Check. You caught no piece of the flop, two high cards hit, and you have two opponents yet to act. Do not bluff here. Check and fold to any bet.

Action: Everyone checks.

Turn: 3♥

Question: Check or bet?

> **Answer:** Check. You should begin to think there is a strong chance nobody has anything. However, you are still first to act and have not connected with the board in any way. So just check.

Action: Your opponents all check.

River: 2♣

Question: Check or bet?

> **Answer:** Bet t75. By checking twice with superior position, your opponents have shown tremendous weakness. It is highly improbable the river deuce improved anyone. And lastly, if you check, you have no chance of winning the pot at showdown with your six-high. Aggression therefore requires you to bluff here, and betting t75, you are getting 2-to-1 on your investment when you will probably be called less than half the time.

Aggressing Post-Flop

Sometimes your transition to mid and high-blind play requires aggressive post-flop play. The section above gave a taste of this post-flop play, and in this section, we consider bigger plays. This usually occurs when you flop a decent made hand or draw from one of the blinds, or hit a speculative or quality hand that is vulnerable.

Hand 2-44

Blinds: t100-t200, 9 players

Your hand: You (t1,500) have K♠5♥ in the big blind.
Action to you: The LAG chip leader (t4,800) limps from MP1 position, gets one loose caller (t2,400), and the small blind (t1,800) completes.

Question: Check or raise?
    Answer: Check. An all-in steal is acceptable, but it is likely you will be called by the big-stacked loose limper, and your marginal hand does poorly heads-up. (There are four players and t800 in the pot.)

Flop: J♣5♦3♠
Action: The small blind checks.

Question: What is your play?
    Answer: Check. Holding mid pair against three opponents, you should not lead out early to act since any bet you make at this $800 pot will be pot-committing due to your relatively short stack. This is problematic since mid pair is not strong enough to shove here with three active opponents and very little information yet as to their possible holdings.

    Your hand is not hopeless, however. Everyone might check, giving you a free chance to improve to two-pair or trips. If anyone does bet this flop, it is most likely to be the initial loose-aggressive limper who is one to your left. And if he does bet, you will have relative position over the other two active players, and you may then decide on your play based upon how these opponents respond to this LAG's bet.

Action: You check. The LAG bets t500, and it is folded back to you.

Question: Fold, call, or raise?
    Answer: Raise all-in. The LAG limper may be on a variety of hands right now: two overcards, any pocket pair (low, mid,

or high), king-queen, ace-x suited, etc. But there is now t1,300 in the pot, your stack is t1,500, and even if he does call and you are behind, you will improve to two pair or better 20 percent of the time. This is a favorable gamble, particularly when you are getting short-stacked relative to the blinds.

If the relative positions were such that other active players remained after your turn, or the bettor was passive, you would be forced to fold. But a big-stacked aggressive player seeing only checks is liable to bet nearly anything; and the betting order placed you heads-up against him post-flop after he bet. It is this piece of luck that you are exploiting with your all-in reraise.

Hand 2-45

Blinds: t50-t100, 7 players

Your hand: You (t1,600) have A♠K♣ on the button.
Action to you: Everyone folds.

Question: What is your play?
    Answer: Make a standard raise of 2½ to 3BB.

Action: You make a standard raise to t300. The small blind folds and the big blind (t2,400) puts in another t200 to call. (There are two players and t650 in the pot.)

Flop: A♦9♦3♦
Action: He checks.

Question: Check or bet?
    Answer: Bet big. You almost certainly have the best hand at the moment. But if another diamond falls, your hand is ruined. Furthermore, the pot is already a sizeable fraction of your stack, and you may be called by a worse hand such as a

weaker ace or K♦X. Force your opponent to surrender the pot immediately or make a pot-committing call with a worse hand.

Hand 2-46

Blinds: t50-t100, 9 players

Your hand: You (t1,800) are the big blind with 8♣2♣.

Action to you: There are three limpers. The small blind completes, and you check. (There are five players and t500 in the pot.)

Flop: J♣8♠3♣

Action: The small blind (t2,100) checks. You check. The first limper (t2,200) bets t300 and gets one call (t4,000) and one fold.

Question: What do you do?

> **Answer:** Move all-in. With a flush draw and a pair — giving you 14 outs twice to improve, you are even money against a hand as strong as A♥J♥. Meanwhile, there is already t1,100 on the table, well over half your stack. Even in the worst outcome, namely that you are called by an opponent with a set of treys, your are still only a 7-to-3 underdog.
>
> This situation is favorable in three respects:

1. You are the aggressor.

2. You are getting an excellent return on your chip investment (better than 3-to-2).

3. You are at least even money against your opponents' most likely best holdings, namely a jack with an overcard

Note that leading out at this flop would also be a viable option. But I prefer the check-raise approach. This is because if you lead out with a pot-sized bet and an opponent raises you for all your chips, you are then forced to fold despite the excellent pot odds, or forfeit your status as aggressor by calling — rarely a desirable move without a very strong hand. The check-raise approach described above allows you to avoid this negative decision, and thus it is the check-raise that we advocate over the lead-out.

Crucial Mid-Blind Concepts

Independent Chip Model (ICM)

Earlier we discussed the difference between chip expected value and sit 'n go equity. The Independent Chip Model (ICM) is a procedure that takes the chip stacks of all remaining players as an input, and produces each player's corresponding equity as an output. Since ICM calculations are lengthy, and you will typically be using software to perform them, it is more important that you understand the basics of the underlying procedure rather than master manually performing the stack-to-equity calculations themselves.

So here is a simple, yet common, example. Suppose there are three players remaining in a 10 player sit 'n go with prizes of $1,000, $600, and $400.[6] Stack sizes are as follows:

> Player A: t5,000
> Player B: t6,500
> Player C: t2,000

If this sit 'n go was winner-take-all, each player's chances of winning could be calculated easily by simply dividing Player X's chip stack by the total chips in play. That is, if these are three average players, their chances of winning are directly proportional to the number of chips they have. The Independent Chip Model

---

[6] (The same logic applies to more players, but we stick with three to make the calculations readable.)

begins by taking this direct proportionality as a given and thus in this example the probability that Player A wins is 0.37.

$$0.37 = \frac{\$5,000}{\$5,000 + \$6,500 + \$2,000}$$

Abbreviating Probability (Player X wins Nth) as Pr(X Nth), we write the corresponding equations:

$$\text{Pr(B 1st)} = \frac{\$6,500}{\$13,500} = 0.48$$

$$\text{Pr(C 1st)} = \frac{\$2,000}{\$13,500} = 0.15$$

Now, the equity of Player X, Eq(X) in this case is:

$$\text{Eq(X)} = \text{Pr(X 1st)}(\$1,000) + \text{Pr(X 2nd)}(\$600) + \text{Pr(X 3rd)}(\$400)$$

This is no different from any expected value calculation. The expected dollar equity of Player X is simply how often he expects to place first multiplied by the reward for first ($1,000), plus the percentage of the time he places second multiplied by the reward for second ($600), and so forth.

Now we know all the rewards in the above equity equation since these are given to us from the beginning. Furthermore, we saw that determining each Pr(X 1st) is accomplished by simple division. So the question becomes what is the probability for each player to finish second or third those times that they do not win?

Let us consider this problem from Player A's perspective. If we knew that Player B was going to win, then we could temporarily ignore B's stack and focus instead on A's present stack versus C's present stack to determine their relative second versus third place finish probabilities. In particular, A has t5,000 at present, C has t2,000, and so if B wins, then A expects to finish second 71 percent of the time. T

$$.71 = \frac{T5,000}{T5,000 + T2,000}$$

Meanwhile, if C wins, A expects to finish second 43 percent of the time (based on similar calculations).

Therefore the probability that A takes second is an expected value calculation of its own which computes to 41 percent.

$$Pr(A\ 2nd) = \big(Pr(B\ 1st)\big)\big(Pr(A\ beats\ C\ for\ 2nd)\big) +$$
$$\big(Pr(C\ 1st)\big)\big(Pr(A\ beats\ B\ for\ 2nd)\big)$$

$$= (0.37)(0.71) + (0.15)(0.43) = 0.41$$

And since A must finish exactly first, second, or third, and all three of these possibilities must sum to a probability of 1, the Pr(A 3rd) computes to 22 percent.

$$Pr(A\ 3rd) = 1 - Pr(A\ 1st) - Pr(A\ 2nd)$$
$$= 1 - 0.37 - 0.41$$
$$= 0.22$$

Applying similar calculations to Players B and C, we get the following finish probabilities:

Player	Stack	Pr(1st)	Pr(2nd)	Pr(3rd)	Equity
A	t5,000	37%	41%	22%	?
B	t6,500	48%	37%	15%	?
C	t2,000	15%	22%	63%	?

We may now plug these values into the equity equation (Eq(X)) derived above to get our Independent Chip Model equities and thereby complete the final column in this table.

$$\text{Equity of Player A} = (0.37)(\$1,000) + (0.41)(\$600) + (0.22)(\$400)$$
$$= \$704$$

Similar calculations give us the dollar equities of Players B and C, and so we now have our official Independent Chip Model stack-to-equity conversions:

Player	Stack	Equity
A	t5,000	$704
B	t6,500	$762
C	t2,000	$534

Such is the basic theory behind the Independent Chip Model.[7] We now consider two ICM commonly asked questions:

1. How should the Independent Chip Model be used?

2. What are the limitations of the Independent Chip Model?

---

[7] For those interested, the first example of ICM type calculations related to poker tournaments appeared in the 1987 edition of *Gambling Theory and Other Topics* by Mason Malmuth.

The answer to the first question is that the Independent Chip Model allows you to think in terms of sit 'n go equity rather than chip expected value. For example, suppose you are considering a t400 all-in call (which will close the action) in a sit 'n go. Then:

$$\text{Equity of calling} = \big(\Pr(\text{you win the hand})\big)\big(\text{Equity after you win}\big)$$
$$+ \big(\Pr(\text{you lose the hand})\big)\big(\text{Equity after you lose}\big)$$

(Technically a term should also be thrown in for the case of a split pot, but we omit this term due to comparative rarity.) The answer to the second question is discussed later in this sub-chapter.

So the Independent Chip Model is what gives you the dollar amount of each equity term in the latter equation. Similarly, if you are considering pushing yourself:

$$\text{Equity of pushing} =$$

$$\big(\Pr(\text{Opponent folds})\big)\big(\text{Equity after winning what is on the table}\big)$$
$$+ \big(\Pr(\text{Opponent calls})\big)\left[\begin{array}{l}\big(\Pr(\text{You win})\big)\big(\text{Equity after win}\big) \\ + \big(\Pr(\text{You lose})\big)\big(\text{Equity after your loss}\big)\end{array}\right]$$

While meanwhile, if you fold:

$$\text{Equity of folding} = \text{Equity of present stack}$$

That is, if you fold, then your stack does not change by hypothesis, and therefore your equity cannot change either.

So the Independent Chip Model gives you the information you need to determine whether calling/pushing versus folding will increase your tournament equity, also known as winning money in the long run. Again, there is plenty of software that will automatically perform these laborious calculations for you. Two excellent programs at the moment are SNG Power Tools and SNG Wizard — all you have to do is select a range of hands that your opponent might reasonably push with (when you are considering calling), or call with (when you are considering pushing), and the software returns your expected equity as output.

An example of a detailed fold/call comparison using the Independent Chip Model is given in the opening problem of the sub-chapter on "Bubble Play" on page 147 in "Part Three: High-Blind Play."

We conclude this topic by addressing the second question: What are the limitations of the Independent Chip Model?

This is a topic of vigorous debate, but there is one very important caveat that must be considered whenever the ICM is used:

> The Independent Chip Model does not take player skill and relative positions into account.

For example, suppose you are an expert sit 'n go player who has been crushing 9 player $109 sit 'n go's. You find yourself at a table with 9 weak players and want to know your starting equity. At the start of the tournament you each have identical chip stacks and therefore identical ICM equities of $100. And yet your equity is certainly higher than $100 since you are superior to your opposition by hypothesis.

Here is a more subtle example. Suppose you have three reckless players to your right and three tight-passive, blind-indefensive opponents on your left. The blinds are high and your stack is large. Then these excellent table conditions make your actual equity considerably higher than the Independent Chip Model suggests, and so you might make a fold ICM-style calculations label as slightly minus-Equity. This would be when, say, a reckless opponent pushes and you have a solid hand.

This declining of a positive equity play can be correct because pursuing a pro-active strategy of ruthless blind-stealing against your tight opponents, while observing your reckless opponents knock each other out from the sidelines, may earn you more money in the long run for the sit 'n go as a whole relative to seizing a slightly positive equity gamble immediately.

Situations like the above are fundamentally judgment calls. Unless you are an experienced player, if the Independent Chip Model suggests that a given move is positive equity, seize a guaranteed edge and make the play.

Defeating Tight-Aggressive Opponents

As you climb in buy-in, you will begin to notice other players with a similarly tight-aggressive strategy. Tend to avoid these players in general, particularly if you know they will be sitting on your right, as they will usually decrease your equity going into the tournament (see "Table Selection" starting on page 235 in "Part Four: Sit 'n Go Career Play" for more on this topic.)

If you are up against another tight-aggressive player, picture yourself playing as him. His general playing style should be similar to yours (by hypothesis). Also, you should try to determine whether he realizes you are a good player and is adjusting accordingly. Determining his perception of you will allow you to think one level above him and thereby gain an edge.

Hand 2-47

Blinds: t200-t400, 7 players

Your hand: You (t3,600) have A♦A♣ in the small blind. The multi-tabling TAG in the big blind has t1,800 after posting.
Action to you: Everyone folds.

Question: Your move?

Answer: Call. This type of player is good enough to attack passivity, but is too busy to analyze your play and realize you are not the limping type. He will reraise all-in often enough that a mere call is your best chance to get all his chips committed before the flop.

If the big blind in the above hand is loose (or anything besides TAG, for that matter), make a small raise instead. In either case, your hand is strong enough heads-up that few flops will be of significant concern.

Hand 2-48

Blinds: t50-t100, 6 players

Your hand: You (t2,100) have K♠J♠ in the cut-off.
Action to you: Everyone folds.

Question: What is your move?

Answer: Make a standard raise of 2½ to 3BB.

Action: You raise to t300. The button folds. The solid tight-aggressive small blind (t2,000) calls. The big blind folds. (There are two players and t650 in the pot.)

Flop: K♦9♥2♥

Action: The small blind checks, and you bet t350 with your top pair. He raises to t750.

Question: Call or fold?

Answer: Fold. The pot is t1,750, and it costs you only t450 to call. But let us think about what your opponent could have. He is tight and aggressive, yet smooth-called a raise out of position pre-flop. This indicates great strength. Then when a king lands, your opponent makes a pot-committing check-raise. This indicates he likes the flop. Would you make this series of plays with any hand that could not beat king-jack at this point? No, and he probably wouldn't either. You will often see two aces if you call, and the times he has queens, jacks, or tens, or is running some type of bluff will not compensate. So fold.

Adjusting to Different Stack Sizes: Mid Blind

Earlier, we mentioned that you should usually push when blind-stealing with under ten big blinds, but avoid pushing with more as the reward becomes too small for the risk of busting out. But anytime you are involved in a hand with a shorter-stacked opponent, your effective stack is his stack. This is because *anything extra you bet goes into a sidepot that you automatically take down*, and this concept is important to remember anytime you play a hand with a shorter-stacked opponent.

For instance, suppose the blinds are t50-t100 and you have t3,800 after posting your small blind. All fold to you, leaving you against the big blind who has t600 after posting. Then if you raise all-in, your effective bet is t700, since even if he calls, the chips you bet beyond his stack you automatically win back. Let us look at two more examples of this concept.

Hand 2-49

Blinds: t100-t200, 7 players

Your hand: You (t5,200) have K♣T♣ on the button. The big blind (1,600) is tight-aggressive, and the small blind is the short stack with t1,100.
Action to you: Everyone folds.

Question: What is your move?

Answer: Raise all-in. Despite having over 25 big blinds, you should push. This is because your effective stack is t1,800, as none of your remaining t3,600 can be involved in this pot. So push instead of the smaller raise you might make against another big stack. A smaller raise is a particular mistake here, as your tight-aggressive nemesis might reraise if he thinks you will potentially fold to a re-steal.

Avoid situations where you are forced to gamble or leave the hand, and in this hand, that entails raising all-in now.

Hand 2-50

Blinds: t100-t200, 8 players

Your hand: You (t2,400) have J♠5♣ in the small blind. The reckless big blind has t150 after posting his t200 big blind.

Question: Fold, call, or raise?

Answer: Raise. First, observe that a call is pot-committing, and so if you decide to play the hand, you may as well raise. Second, note that winning or losing this all-in will not have any significant bearing on your winning chances, so you should play only if you are being offered a good, positive cEV gamble. You must answer two questions: What are the pot odds? and what type of favorite/underdog do I figure to be?

1.   **Pot Odds:** Even a weak big blind will typically realize he cannot fold his t200 blind for another t150 regardless of his holding, so the pot is effectively t450 (t300 in blinds + t150 in his remaining stack). Meanwhile, it costs you t250 to call (t100 to match his big blind, plus

the extra t150 in his stack). So you are getting 9-to-5, or a little worse than 2-to-1.

2.   **Odds of Winning:** A jack-high is an average hand, so figure to be close to 50 percent. (Pokerstove puts you at 47-to-53. See "Appendix E: Your Hand Versus a Random Hand" on page 259 to see how various hands hold up pre-flop against a random hand.)

So in this hand you are being offered nearly 2-to-1 odds on a gamble for which you should be close to even money to win. Therefore you should play the hand, i.e., raise.

Mid-Blind Play: Summary

During mid-blind play, use a tight-aggressive style and stick with premium hands, speculative hands with a cheap price and favorable conditions, or hands that have solid steal or re-steal prospects. And perhaps most importantly, make sure you are comfortable attacking passivity as the blinds rise and you need to make a move. Recognize when weak players are limping and will not stand up to an attack, come over the top of aggressive players making obvious steal-raises, and otherwise seize any exploitable tendencies you notice in your opponents.

Again, the winning style is tight-aggressive. During low-blind play, the tight/cautious aspect was emphasized. But during mid-blind play, a less cautious style is advocated to stay in the game Now we move to an unrelenting aggression necessary for a high win percentage when the high blinds alone create a significant pot to fight for.

Let us see what this type of play entails.

Part Three

High-Blind Play

High-Blind Play

Introduction

As the table gets short-handed and the blinds rise, you will have to play many hands and be very aggressive. There is also less room for creativity. Whereas there are alternate ways to play many low and mid-blind hands, high-blind play usually lends itself to a single correct answer: Commit all your chips if doing so will increase your equity, and fold otherwise. This is because unless you and the remaining active players have large stacks, smaller raises tend to require so many chips that they pot-commit you to the hand should your opponent call or reraise. And when you are pot-committed anyway, you may as well push yourself in the first place.

When should you fold? When should you push? And when should you try a different play? These are the questions we will be answering in "Part Three: High-Blind Play," and it all begins with one key principle.

High-Blind Strategy

The Fundamental Theorem of Sit 'n Go High-Blind Play

Without further ado:

> Never allow yourself to get blinded out.

Let us be more specific. If you have a stack between 3 to 5BB, and you let the blinds hit you rather than make a move earlier, then you have broken the cardinal rule and allowed yourself to be blinded out.

The underlying principle behind this concept is that the minimum stack you must have for a reasonable chance to steal the blinds without a fight is 3BB. Even this is a low number, since the big blind must pay 2BB to match your raise with a pot of 4.5BB. He is therefore getting better than 2-to-1, and is probably correct to call with any two cards from a cEV perspective.

Of course, you cannot assume your opponents will play rationally. Some will fold a marginal hand to an all-in raise of 2BB (a clear error, as discussed below), while others will call a 6BB push with a weak jack-high. As an empirical assumption then, you might get everyone to fold with 3BB, but probably not with less.

This minimum-fold threshold is dependent not only on the player(s) being pushed upon, but also on the level of the blinds. For example, if you suffer a crippling loss during t20-t40, it will be very difficult to steal the blinds with a stack less than around t200 (5BB). However, a short-stacked big blind may well fold to a raise of t800 to t900 during t200-t$400 bubble play. So always try to determine how large a stack you must have to maintain blind-stealing power at your particular table and game stage. If this stack size is different from 3BB, adjust accordingly.

Continuing with the 3BB assumption, it follows that with a stack over 5BB you can let the blinds hit you and still conceivably steal the following orbit. With under 3BB, you are already blinded out. And with 3 to 5BB, you must act.

For example, suppose the blinds are t200-t400, and your stack is:

Case No. 1: You have a stack of t2,000 or more. If the blinds hit you, you will still have at least t1,400 (3.5BB), enough to make a legitimate steal attempt the following orbit. So while you should still seize any positive equity situation should one arise, let the blinds hit you rather than force a play.

Case No. 2: You have a stack less than t1,200. In this case, you are already blinded out. Even if no intermediate player wants to challenge you for your relatively short stack, the big blind is getting considerably better than 2-to-1 on his call. For example, if you have t1,000, then he must call t600 on a pot of t1,600, giving him 8-to-3. These are good enough odds that he will have a positive cEV calling with

even if he knew you had

Even if your opponents have no knowledge of pre-flop all-in probabilities or pot odds, the big blind (or another opponent) may intuitively see that he has the opportunity to bust you, winning your stack and the blinds, via a minimal investment. So at this point, your tournament life usually hinges on one or more gambles going your way before you can even regain your status as a legitimate contender.

Your tournament equity plummets when you hit Case No. 2, and it is to be avoided at all costs. This brings us to Case No. 3.

Case No. 3: You have a stack between t1,200 and t2,000. If you let the blinds pass, you will now be in (or very near) the dreaded Case No. 2. You must avoid this situation at all costs, and the way to do this is to make a move before the blinds hit you. Make a move at all costs rather than get blinded out.

Many will concede this conclusion in theory, but then object: "But every time I get short-stacked, it seems every hand I'm dealt is either trash or I have someone else raising before me. What am I supposed to do, just push with nothing?" Yes.

> You should push with nothing rather than get blinded out.

Let us assume that anyone with a hand in the top fifth of starting hands will call your steal-raise of 3 to 5BB. Then if you were to blindly push two cards dealt you, you would win 36 percent of those times you were called. Read this again: A random hand will win more often than once in three, on average, against a legimimate hand. Those are about the same odds as completing an open-ended straight draw or flush draw after the flop — not so bad.

Indeed, if you make such a blind all-in, it is not a bluff, rather a semi-bluff. This is because:

1. Your opponent(s) may fold.

2. Your hand might actually be the favorite heading into the flop. (You may be pushing with

after all).

3. If you are an underdog, you may always improve to beat your opponent over the next five cards (which, as stated above, you will do on average more than one-third of the time).

The reason that two random cards win so often over much better hands is that high cards significantly outnumber pairs. Therefore the common worst-case scenario is pushing with two low cards and getting called by two high cards. But even in this case, the high cards are only about a 2-to-1 favorite. The cases where you are facing an overpair are roughly offset by those times your in-the-dark push is with a hand that is a favorite or only a slight underdog.

How Not to Get Blinded Out

With a stack of around 3 to 5BB, the best strategy to avoid getting blinded out is to pick a player who will be the big blind within three or so hands before the big blind hits you, and then push in the dark (but pretend to look) on him if no favorable situation arises earlier. You want this opponent to be as tight a caller as possible and have a short to moderate stack. We will consider a concrete example of this process below.

For now, let us ask: If you are pushing a random hand with a short stack and are called X percent of the time, how big can X be for the push still to be profitable? For instance, if you believed X was 100 percent you would have no chance of stealing, whereas X = 0 percent would guarantee you a free blind-steal.

So if your stack is t300, the blinds are t50-t100, and assuming the caller is always the big blind (which will make the push appear less profitable than it actually is), and you expect to win 36 percent of the time when called:

$$(1 - X)(t150) + (X)\left[(.36)(t350) - (.64)(t300)\right] \leq 0 \Rightarrow$$
$$150 - 213.4X \leq 0 \Rightarrow$$
$$X \geq 0.72$$

So if you believe there is at least a 100 - 72 = 28 percent chance everyone will fold, a blind push becomes positive cEV. However, there is almost never a situation when you should expect to be called more often than 30 percent of the time pushing with a stack of 3BB or higher, particularly if the big blind in the hand is tight and shorter-stacked. So rather than face a certain plummet in equity, take your chances with a bluff-steal.

Hand 3-1

Blinds: t200-t400, 7 players

Your hand: You (t1,300) are on the button. The remaining players, beginning with your leftmost, are:

Player	Chips	Style
L1	t2,300	tight-passive
L2	t1,600	loose
L3	t6,300	loose-aggressive
L4	t3,500	not much known
L5	t2,100	tight-aggressive
L6	t2,700	loose

Therefore L1 and L2 are the current small and big blinds, respectively, and L6 will be big blind immediately before you.

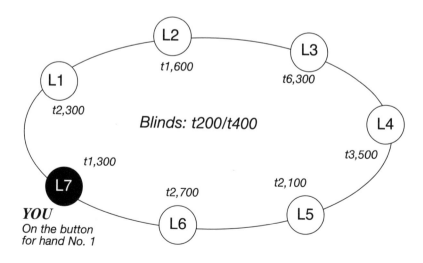

Question: If no reasonable stealing situation arises, at what point should you force a move and simply push in the dark?

    Answer: Push three hands from the present, when L5 is the big blind. He is tight, has a stack small enough so that a call and loss against you would cripple him, and he gets the blind only two hands before you (so the only potential opportunity you miss is the one hand when the loose L6 is big blind).

    While other players besides the big blind may still contest your blind-push, they will usually need a legitimate hand. So unless you are at a particularly reckless table, you should pay most attention to the player who is in the big blind when you push.

Let us see how this might actually play out.

Hand No. 1: L2 (t1,200) is big blind. You have 5♠4♠ on the button. All fold to L6 who raises to t1,400.

    Question: Call or fold?

    Answer: Fold. Low suited connectors are a fine pushing hand. This is because when pushing, your cards only matter if you are called. Two low cards will rarely be dominated, and suited connectors add considerably to your winning chances against common calling hands. Please see "Appendix D: Pre-flop Hand Probabilities" on page 257 for a more quantitative elaboration. So absent a raise by L6, you should push. But with over 3BB and 5 hands before you are hit by the big blind, calling as a certain underdog should be avoided.

Hand No. 2: L3 (t5,900) is big blind. You have J♠2♣. All fold to you in the cut-off.

> **Question:** Push or fold?
>
> **Answer:** Fold. A loose player with an enormous stack, who may even explicitly realize you are desperate, is not a good candidate to push on with two other potential callers and a weak hand.

Hand No. 3: L4 (t3,100) is big blind, and you have 7♣3♥. All fold to you in the hijack.

> **Question:** Push or fold?
>
> **Answer:** Fold. You have no hand, and the blinds are both bigger stacks liable to call.

Hand No. 4: L5 (t1,700) is big blind. You are MP2. L6 folds.

> **Question:** Push or fold?
>
> **Answer:** Push. It does not matter what you have. Cover up the screen with your left hand and raise all-in with your right. You will win over half your stack uncontested at least half the time, and when someone does call, you will be better than a 2-to-1 underdog, on average, at a point when you need to gamble anyway.

Two more observations:

1. If there is no good candidate for a big blind to push on, or there is such a candidate but a player between you and this blind pushes earlier during the hand (such as if L6 had raised UTG in Hand No. 4 above), tend to push the last possible hand in the dark — when you are under-the-gun — rather than getting blinded out if you feel there is any reasonable chance of an uncontested blind-steal.

2. If you have any opportunity to push earlier and not put yourself in a situation where a blind-push is your best option,

so much the better. For instance, in the example above, if you had been dealt J♠T♠ in Hand No. 2, or any other reasonable pushing/calling situation arises, seize it and avoid the need to push in the dark entirely.

Hand 3-2

Blinds: t200-t400, 7 players

Your hand: You (t1,200) have T♣9♠ as MP1.
Action to you: Everyone folds to you.

Question: What is your play?
> **Answer:** Push all-in. In two hands you start getting blinded out. Avoid this. Everyone could well fold to your bet, and if not, you need to gamble anyway. Folding guarantees you stay alive, but mere survival is worth little when you are a couple of hands away from being crippled. Recognize when you have to gamble, and be willing to push some marginal hands when you do.

Your cards only matter if you get called, and as we stated, even getting called rarely makes you worse than a 2-to-1 underdog.

High-Blind Re-Steals

No play is as brutally aggressive as the high-blind re-steal. This move, applied at the right times, will become one of the most crucial moves in your arsenal. Let us look at some examples.

Hand 3-3

Blinds: t300-t600, 5 players

Your hand: You (t3,800) have K♠T♣ in the small blind. The button is a loose player who has been routinely min-raising during high-blind play. The big blind has t4,200, UTG is minuscule-stacked, and the tight-passive cut-off is the chip leader with t6,000.

Action to you: All fold to the button (t5,100) who min-raises.

Question: Do you fold, call, or raise?

> **Answer:** Reraise all-in. Your raise will be to t4,100, around 3.5 times the button's bet, which puts a lot of pressure on him. If he calls and loses, he will go from a major contender to being on the verge of elimination with under 2BB. In addition, you have a decent hand, particularly for short-handed high-blind play. The button's raise is almost certainly steal rather than value — he is a loose player raising his standard amount with position.
>
> If you get a fold, you will win t2,100, over 50 percent of your stack. With t5,900, you will be about tied with the passive (i.e., weak) chip leader and in solid position to aggress mercilessly near the bubble and place yourself in position to place first. And should the button call, while this is certainly not what you want, you may still win a huge pot with your two high cards putting you solidly in the lead.

Many players will recognize the benefits of such aggressive play, yet still hesitate, not wanting to take such a big risk with a decent-sized stack before the money. But it is precisely this instinct that makes such a play correct since many of your opponents will want to avoid a certain gamble with their big stacks at all costs.

You cannot play frightened poker, particularly late in a tournament. Remember, when you play a cautious game during the early stages, you maximize your chances of making it late into the tournament. But the cost is generally a smaller stack than your loose opponents late in the tournament. You must not coast along and get blinded out before the money or in third place. You want to make an aggressive stand to accumulate chips when your fellow opponents are tightening up their calls near the money, thereby maximizing your chances of winning the tournament.

After all, one first is much better than two-thirds. You win 25 percent more, and forfeit one less rake and time investment.

Hand 3-4

Blinds: t200-t400, 8 players

Your hand: You (t3,200) have K♠Q♠ on the button. The blinds rise to t300-t600 in 1 minute.

Action to you: The TAG chip leader (t4,200) raises to t1,000 from the cutoff.

Question: What is your move?
> **Answer:** Re-steal all-in. Your opponent's raise is a probable steal raise, you have a decent hand, and your bet is just large enough that he will probably fold without a real hand. Be the aggressor in this key pot with an all-in re-steal.

This last point regarding raise size is crucial. Let us modify the above hand to see why.

Hand 3–5

Blinds: t200-t400, 8 players

Your hand: You (t2,300) have K♠Q♠ on the button. The blinds are about to rise.

Action to you: The TAG chip leader (t5,300) raises to t1,100 from the hijack seat.

Question: What is your move?

> **Answer:** Fold. Your opponent's raise should still be classified as steal, and you have the identical decent hand. But here you cannot hope your big-stacked opponent will fold. You are raising barely double his bet, offering him better than 3-to-1 odds on a call. Even if he has a weak hand, he will almost certainly call rather than fold for another t1,200. Lacking the fold possibility, a reraise here is simply a guaranteed gamble for all your chips. Your hand is not strong enough to warrant such a gamble while you still have enough chips to blind-steal.

The Ante: Strategic Adjustments

When deciding whether to attack the blinds or make a big call, particularly when an all-in is involved, you need a measure of how urgently you need to make a move. Attack (or risk all your chips) too early, and you risk an unnecessary bust-out. Attack too late, and you have esentially been blinded out. There are two measures commonly used to place stack size into context.

1. The BB measure. Divide your present stack size by the present size of the big blind, and this is your BB. For example, if you are playing 4-handed with blinds of t100-t200 and a t25 ante, and your stack is t1,600, then you have a stack of t1,600/t200 = 8BB.

2. The Harrington M measure. Divide your present stack size by the size of the starting pot, and this is your M. Taking the hand from above, the starting pot is t300 (from the blinds) + t100 (from the antes) = t400, and so your M is t1,600/t400 = 4.

A rough guideline for comparing these measures is as follows:

- If you have a BB of 10 or under, and you intend to play the hand, you should raise all-in.

- If you have an M of 5 or under, and you intend to play the hand, you should raise all-in.

- If you have a BB of 5 or under, you should be looking for any opportunity to open-push rather than get blinded out.

- If you have an M of 3 or under, you should be looking for any opportunity to open-push rather than get blinded out.

These statements are certainly not absolute. They are rather approximate guidelines that depend on the situation. The 10 and 5BB cut-offs are discussed elsewhere in this book. For more on M discussion, please consult *Harrington on Hold 'em; Volume II: The Endgame.*

In this book, our default is the BB measure. This choice is for several reasons. First, it is more immediate to calculate, both at the present moment and when looking ahead to the next blind increase. Second is convention. Sit 'n go discussion has generally centered around the BB count. Lastly, sit 'n go antes tend to be much less significant than multi-table tournament antes. Not only are they typically smaller in proportion to the blinds, but by the time the ante comes into play, the table is usually short-handed, so the sum of the antes is considerably less than it would be at a 9 player multi-table tournament table.

As a corollary to this latter assertion on ante significance, when playing a multi-table tournament, antes play a significant role in late-stage play and *must* be accounted for. Thus in these events, the concept of M becomes very useful.

(Note: The basis of the following hand is *Harrington on Hold 'em; Volume II: The Endgame*, Hand 9-10.)

Hand 3-6

Blinds: t6,000-t12,000, t2,000 ante, 9 players

Your hand: You (t135,000) are UTG with K♦Q♥.

Question: What is your play?

    Answer: Raise all-in. Using the BB measure, you have easily over 10BB, and would be foolish to push under-the-gun at a full table holding K♦Q♥. But in this situation, 9 players contributing t2,000 each in ante money adds a dead t18,000 (!) to the pot. So not only will your stack dwindle at a much quicker rate with a forced t2,000 ante contribution per hand, but there is vastly more to win — in this case, double — through a blind-steal. So the correct thinking for this hand is that you have an M of between 3 and 4 (t135,000/t36,000), and also a decent hand, and so you should push.

But this is a book on sit 'n go's, so we ask: When do antes force you to look beyond the BB measure in sit 'n go play? There are two primary situations:

1. When the ante comes into play and the table is still mostly full (most common in non-turbo or other longer structure sit 'n go's), and

2. When you are considering a very borderline steal or call when thought of in BB terms.

    Here are a couple of examples.

Hand 3-7

Blinds: t100-t200, t25 ante, 8 players

Your hand: You (t3,100) are UTG with A♣J♠. The big blind is tight-passive.

Question: What is your play?

   Answer: Raise to t500. Without antes, I would suggest folding A♣J♠ in this position unless the table is very tight. But with the ante, the starting pot is t500 instead of t300. Therefore a successful blind-steal represents a vastly greater chip increase of 67 percent, and you are getting even money on the steal investment (risking t500 to win t500).

The ante money makes it as if there is an extra t200 blind sitting out there, but with nobody to defend it. Consequently, perhaps, few sit 'n go players adjust well to the new pot odds subsequent to the ante. For instance, the tight-passive big blind will be getting better than 3-to-1 (t1,000-to-t300) on his call, but will most likely — as an empirical observation — defend his blind with a similar range of hands to the ante-less situation where he is getting a more modest 8-to-3. But you should adjust your playing style to account for the ante, just as the big blind from this hand will usually fail to do when he is facing a raise.

Hand 3-8

Blinds: t200-t400, t75 ante, 6 players

Your hand: You (t5,100) have 7♦3♠ in the big blind.
Action to you: All fold to the solid player on the button (t1,400) who raises all-in with the shortest stack. The small blind folds.

Question: Call or fold?

Answer: Call. Without the ante, the pot is t1,400 (Villain's bet) + t600 (blind money) = t2,000. It costs you t1,000 to call and so you are getting exactly 2-to-1. As discussed in the sections on calling all-in bets, this would normally be a very borderline situation as you will, on average, be a 2-to-1 underdog against your opponent's wide pushing range.

In this case, calling has the potential to knock out a good player and establish a blind defensive image, yet offers you no chip advantage (let alone an equity edge). So I might call or fold, depending on other factors, such as the utility of the extra thousand chips in out-aggressing the table. It would depend.

But with an ante, you should definitely call. This is because the pot is now padded with an extra t450 of dead money. By the 2 to 1 rule in our "Calling All-In" chapters, your nearly 5-to-2 odds swing this borderline situation into one where calling is now the superior play.

In summary, always adjust for the new odds created by the introduction of an ante when deciding whether to fold versus blind-steal, call an all-in versus fold, and so forth. Depending on the limit, your opponents either won't make this adjustment or won't do it well. So this is one of the edges you can pick up in some sit 'n go's.

Critical
High-Blind Concepts

Bubble Play

Bubble play represents a unique opportunity for the solid player to accumulate chips through aggression. This is because many players don't want to risk a lot of chips just outside the money, and so opponents will often fold even strong hands rather than face a guaranteed gamble for their entire equity.

Recall that this equity is much higher than it would be if this opponent had the same chip stack during full table play since the elimination of even a single player automatically places him in the money.

We begin with an example of how big a fold can be correct on the bubble when you face a guaranteed gamble for a substantial amount of equity. (The basis for the following hand is *Harrington on Hold 'Em; Volume III: The Workbook*, Problem 38.)

Hand 3–9

Blinds: t200-t400, t25 ante, 4 players

Your hand: You (t5,000) have Q♠Q♣ in the big blind.
Action to you: Pre-flop: The reckless UTG (t5,000) pushes all-in.
   You believe this push is consistent with any ace, pocket pair, or two face cards. The button (t1,500) and small blind (t2,000) both fold.

Question: Call or fold?

> **Answer:** Fold. Calling and losing is a disaster: your vast equity drops to 0. Meanwhile, if you call and win, a substantial amount of the equally vast equity UTG loses goes not to you, but to your short-stacked opponents.

Let us be more concrete, using the ICM procedure to approximate equities. Suppose you are playing a $109 sit 'n go. Before this hand arises, we have the following equities:

Player	Chip Count	Equity
Under the Gun	t5,000	$323
Button	t1,500	$152
Small Blind	t2,000	$195
You	t5,000	$323

If you call and win, the new equities will be as follows:

Player	Chip Count	Equity
Under-the-gun	t0	$0
Button	t1,500	$267
Small Blind	t2,000	$289
You	t10,000	$444

And if you call and lose:

Player	Chip Count	Equity
Under-the-gun	t10,000	$444
Button	t1,500	$267
Small Blind	t2,000	$289
You	t0	$0

So of that $323 in equity that you and your UTG opponent are gambling with, the winner will gain only $121. The rest goes to the short-stacks, who benefit tremendously. This mathematical conclusion correlates with the great pleasure any button or small blind would feel after watching two big stacks collide, thereby ensuring a money finish.

So how good a hand would you need to call a t5,000 all-in push here? When you have Q♠Q♣ in the above hand, you are a 70-to-30 favorite over your opponent's estimated pushing range (from the freeware *Pokerstove*), and so your expected equity *decreases* by $12.20.

$$-\$12.20 = (.3)(-\$323) + (.7)(\$121)$$

that is calling costs you about $12 on average.

You would actually need precisely kings or aces for a positive equity call — with kings you are a 74 percent favorite and so just make the cutoff with a $6 expectation:

$$\$6 = (.26)(-\$323) + (.74)(\$121)$$

There are two lessons here:

1. You do not want to be the one calling an all-in on the bubble unless you have a significant edge, or you are shorter-stacked

relative to the blinds with a strong hand and must make a move to avoid getting blinded out.

2. If you push all-in on the bubble, you are offering your opponent a vastly inferior wager than had you made this same push during non-bubble play, and so he is correct to fold many hands he would normally call with. While few of your opponents will go so far as to discard Q♠Q♣ pre-flop, even a loose and ignorant player strongly wants to finish in the money, and so will tighten up his calling requirements considerably when you push on him. Even if your stack is only enough to damage, yet not eliminate an opponent, he will still frequently tighten significantly.

The surprising result of our

fold hand can therefore be exploited:

> When other players will call with comparatively few hands, so should you aggress with a wider array of hands.

Our hand examples to follow will illustrate this concept in greater detail.

But first, note that earning an above-average stack during bubble play also allows you to greatly increase your proportion of first place finishes when you do win money. And the decrease in your in-the-money (ITM) finishes from busting out at the bubble is not substantial, as a dry run of cards and others' survival may well combine to knock out you out in fourth place even if you "play it safe."

Now suppose the blinds are t200-t400, the table is 4-handed, and the LAG chip leader folds to you on the button. You and the blinds all have about t1,600. Should you push or fold?

You do not need to know your cards to answer "Push" here. Go all-in with any two. If not, you will be blinded out on the bubble. Meanwhile, neither of your opponents will call such an entire-equity gamble without some sort of legitimate hand. So keep in mind that:

> Most players are strongly averse to gambling for all their chips when any other player getting eliminated places them automatically in the money.

As we have seen above, this aversion is largely correct, and can be observed in players of all styles.

This means that very often your bubble raise will win the blinds uncontested. Even if called, two random cards will beat a top hand roughly one-third of the time (see "Appendix E: Your Hand Versus a Random Hand" on page 259), with such wins putting you in position to attack unmercifully with a big stack. And if you fail to push in this hand, then you will either have to push against a big-stacked LAG blind liable to call with many holdings, or fall to a crippled t800 after the blinds do their dirty work. So you will often place fourth anyway if you fold in this spot.

Remember, besides the opportunity to take advantage of strongly risk-averse opponents, the alternative — remaining in the tournament with a very low stack — is a comparatively invaluable survival. It is not like early in a tournament, where walking away will always leave you with more opportunities to accumulate chips and build back. Survival here only means a prolonged elimination in third or fourth unless you catch a lucky run of cards.

So you should often play your situation and opponents, rather than your cards, in high-blind play and bubble play in particular.

Hand 3–10

Blinds: t300–t600, 4 players

Your hand: You (t3,800) have 9♠8♠ and are first to act. The big blind has t6,000 after posting, and the button and small blind each have around t5,000. Play has tightened since the bubble.

Question: Fold, call, or raise?

Answer: Raise all-in. You may follow one of two paths at this critical juncture: high-blind bubble aggression to win, or bubble passivity to maximize your chances of third place. The big blind has you covered, but even if he is loose, he will not want to risk a crippling blow that will markedly damage his chances of moneying if he loses.

If you do get called, this is not a catastrophe for two reasons:

1. The alternative is to let the blinds hit you, thereby becoming more short-stacked and losing substantial equity relative to your present stack (which is large enough to severely threaten each of the remaining stacks).

2. Your mid-high suited connectors will win a full 41 percent of the time against premium high cards such as ace-king, and even though they are worse than a 3-to-1 underdog against an overpair, you will face such a holding under 10 percent of the time. In the much more probable event that nobody has a premium hand, expect to take down these monster blinds without a fight.

High-blind all-in steals, such as the example above, are a common way to exploit favorable bubble conditions, but smaller steals are still highly effective in a mid-blind bubble situation.

Hand 3-11

Blinds: t75-t150, 4 players

Your hand: You (t4,500) are UTG with J♥T♣. Your opponents are similarly-stacked, and there has been little re-stealing.

Question: What is your move?

    Answer: Raise to t375. Few players want to get involved in a potentially big pot at the bubble, and you have a reasonable hand in case of a call. Look to play many pots in situations such as these, raising two to three times the big blind with any decent hand when other players are visibly looking to avoid confrontation.

Hand 3-9

Blinds: t300-t600, 4 players

You have: You (t3,600) have 2♠2♣ in the small blind.
Action to you: All fold to the loose button (t4,400) who makes a characteristic min-raise.

Question: What is your move?

    Answer: Reraise all-in. Do not reason, "It is terrible to go out on the bubble, and some loose opponents call big reraises without premium hands." It *is* terrible to bust out fourth, and even loose opponents tend to realize this. It is quite likely he will fold rather than risk a nearly stack-sized t2,700 on top, and if he does call, your hand could even be a small favorite if he is playing overcards. Taking the t2,100 on the table represents an enormous gain as it increases your stack by well over 50 percent, and you now will be in a position to terrorize the table through aggressive play when everyone else is tightening up.

Again, note that if you push and get called you may still win a very large pot, and if you fold, you may still finish outside the money. Indeed, it is very easy to ignore opportunities such as this one, and then greatly wish you had seized them later. With t300-t600 blinds and 4 players, you must pay t900 per orbit, or even more with antes. Therefore you will have under 3BB in chips left in 8 hands or fewer. It is not uncommon to get unplayable cards or face a prior all-in for eight straight hands. So not only are you putting yourself in position to collect many chips now, thereby putting yourself in solid position to place first once 3-way play occurs, but you are also safeguarding yourself from getting blinded out fourth.

When you do become chip leader during the bubble, one important principle is that another player will fold almost any hand to a tournament-risking all-in rather than allow a short-stacked opponent the opportunity to coast into the money. You should exploit this tendency mercilessly. Let us consider one such situation.

Hand 3-13

Blinds: t300-t600, 4 players

Your hand: You (t11,000) have 5♥2♣ on the button. The blinds each have around t4,000.

Action to you: The cut-off (t1,000) folds.

Question: What is your move?

    Answer: Push all-in. Unless one of the blinds has a monster (say TT — AA, AJ-AK), both will fold rather than gamble with you and risk elimination when the minuscule stack is about to be blinded out the next hand. This is an almost risk-free opportunity to collect t900, and you should seize it regardless of your cards.

    If you do get a call and do not draw out, you will still be second in chips with strong chances of finishing in the money. But be careful that you are pushing on the correct opponent. Suppose we switch the stacks of the cutoff and big blind from the previous hand. This would change the situation drastically.

Hand 3-14

Blinds: t300-t600, 4 players

Your Hand: You (t11,000) have 7♠4♣ on the button. The small blind has t4,000 and the big blind has t1,000.

Action to you: The cut-off (t3,400) folds.

Question: What is your move?

    Answer: Fold. The big blind now has only t1,000 after posting, and will therefore call with many hands rather than forfeit the pot-committing blind money. Meanwhile, your hand is trash. Not only do you not want to throw away chips with an inferior hand against a likely call, but you do not want to be exposed blind-stealing with a trash hand such as 7-high, as it may encourage opponents to call your future steal raises.

This hand brings us to our next idea.

High-Blind Stack Variation

When the blind you are pushing on has a significantly different stack than yours, you must determine how his particular stack size might influence his decision. As stated before, this effect is most important when considering smaller stacks. Players may loosen up with a big stack, but it does not affect their fundamental style of playing. For instance, a tight big blind is usually about as likely to fold to your 4BB steal-raise with a big stack than a normal one. And a player willing to gamble with a normal stack is certainly willing to gamble with a big stack, but usually not noticeably more so.

Players do tend to adjust more to smaller stacks. Most will (correctly) call more liberally when left with only 2 to 3 blinds or fewer after posting. A blind-steal is fundamentally a semi-bluff — your opponent could fold, or if he calls, you may draw out on him — or possibly even have the best hand at the moment.

So while the penalty for losing your chips is less than the penalty to your short-stacked opponent for losing his, he may be more liberal in calling since he is about to be blinded out anyway. Tend to be more literal in such situations raising with any above average hand — 22+, Ax, Kx, Qx, T9s+, and JTo+.

Hand 3-15

Blinds: t300-t600, 5 players

Your hand: You (t2,800) have 5♠4♠ on the button. The big blind (t5,200) is tight, and the small blind (t2,500) has been inactive.

Action to you: The first two players fold.

Question: What is your move?

 Answer: Raise all-in. Force them to surrender the t900 — 30 percent of your stack — sitting on the table, or gamble against a hand which is only a 3-to-2 underdog against even most premium hands. The big blind may have you out-stacked, but that does not mean he wants to give away chips.

Now suppose we keep everything the same in this hand, but change the big blind's stack to t900 after posting. In this case you should fold. The big blind is getting nearly 3-to-1 (t2,400-to-t900 or 8-to-3) on his call, and is therefore correct to do so with any two cards. Even if he is risk averse and ignorant of pot odds, it is intuitive that the blind itself is pot-committing here, and so he will usually call with almost any two cards. And while 5♠4♠ is rarely a big underdog, it almost cannot be a favorite (you would have to be up against a 32, 42, 43, or an inferior 5-high).

So by pushing against the short-stacked big blind, you will probably pay t1,500 to go to showdown as an underdog to potentially win t1,800. Losing drops you down to a damaged t1,300, and so a fold is your best play.

Let us look again at these two five-four suited t300-t600 hands, but now change your hand to K♠2♣, still on the button. You should be less inclined to push against the tight big-stacked big blind, yet more inclined to do so when he is small-stacked. This is because a weak king-high is now favored over the big blind's random hand, yet drops significantly in value against the premium high cards and pairs you will be up against should a tight opponent call.

This observation is also of value in heads-up play. Suppose you know your opponent will push with any reasonable holding, yet only call with a decent hand. Then while you would probably push with 5♠4♠, usually taking the blinds and occasionally gambling as a 3-to-2 underdog on average, you would rarely call as an almost certain underdog.

Hand 3-16

Blinds: t200-t400, 7 players

Your hand: You (t1,400) have 6♠5♠ on the button. The small blind and big blind have t2,300 and t220 after posting, respectively.

Action to you: Everyone folds.

Question: What is your move?

Answer: Fold. With 3½ blinds and suited connectors, normally you would push. But the big blind will almost certainly call after posting his pot-committing blind, and so you figure to gamble as an underdog with your low suited connectors. Wait for a better hand (such as a weak king in this situation) or a hand where everyone might fold.

The Stop 'n Go

Suppose you have a solid hand and are facing a pot-committing raise. You have decided to play the hand, but there is no chance a pre-flop reraise will get your opponent to fold. Then you should consider a "stop 'n go." Merely call the pre-flop raise, and then bet the remainder of your chips at the flop regardless of what comes. This play works best if you are first to act post-flop since your opponent's inability to bet prior to your all-in gives you added fold equity — chips won due to the possibility of your opponent folding.

Your opponent might fold to a small bet if the flop completely misses him. Then you have the potential to win pots when neither of you has anything that you might otherwise lose, such as in a high card battle.

Hand 3-17

Blinds: t100-t200, 9 players

Your hand: You (t700) are the big blind with K♣Q♥.
Action to you: 5 players fold. The loose button (t2,600) min-raises t400. The small blind folds.

Question: What is your move?
   Answer: Call with the intention of pushing the remainder of your stack regardless of the flop. Being short-stacked with a solid hand, you must gamble and hope for the best rather than stay in against many opponents with a nearly blinded-out stack. However, your opponent cannot possibly fold pre-flop against such a modest raise — he must put in another t500 for a pot of t1,400 when you raise.

   If your opponent misses the flop, then you may pick up a pot that you would otherwise lose after a pre-flop call if your opponent folds a low ace or other card that would have paired had he stayed in. Even though he will often call at the flop with nothing but a high card, you have nothing to lose by trying to induce a post-flop fold when your pre-flop reraise will be called with certainty.

Hand 3-18

Blinds: t200-t400

Your hand: You (t785) have Q♣5♠ in the small blind.
Action to you: All fold to the loose button (t4,800) who limps. The tight big blind has t2,100.

Question: What is your play?
    Answer: Raise all-in (t985 total). You have no chance of getting the button to fold pre-flop, so a stop n' go sounds like the best option. But if you push now, the big blind may fold for another t585, thereby contributing t400 in pseudo-dead money to the pot. Take a certain gamble against the button rather than letting the big blind see a free flop with his valuable t400 in chips.

Implicit Collusion

    Suppose there is a multi-way pot where at least one player is all-in. Each remaining player gains equity from any other player busting out. "Implicit collusion" refers to the still-active players having an unspoken agreement to check the hand down, thereby maximizing the odds that the all-in player(s) bust.

    The rationale is that even if you bet/raise with the current best hand, you may knock out an opponent who would have improved to take down the pot over the all-in player's potentially decent holding. Then both active players (as well as everyone else at the table) lose the equity they would otherwise have gained through the third player's elimination.

    Implicit collusion is often the correct path to take in such all-in situations, but there are three noteworthy exceptions:

1.   The pot is large, and you have a hand that is very likely to be best now, but could easily be outdrawn. For instance, if the pot is half your stack and you have top pair on a board of nine-five-deuce, you cannot give a free card to your still-active opponent(s).

2.   There is a significant sidepot between you and the other active player(s), and you think a bet is likely to take down the sidepot. For instance, suppose the cutoff raises 2BB, the button calls for his remaining 0.5BB, and you and the small

blind call as well. Then the main pot is 2BB, while the side pot is 6BB. If you think a bet will knock out the other active players, go ahead and attack.

3. You have the nuts or close to it and are betting for value.

Hand 3-19

Blinds: t300-t600, 4 players

Your hand: You (t6,000) have 9♠6♠ in the big blind.
Action to you: The cutoff (t6,000) folds. The button raises all-in for t850. The small blind (t6,300) calls.

Question: What is your move?
> **Answer:** Call the extra t250. Folding is out of the question due to the pot odds (t2,300-to-t250), and note that if you do raise, this extra amount is going into an empty sidepot. That is, the main pot would be t2,550, and this pot is between you, the button, and the all-in small blind. But if you raise, the raised amount enters an empty sidepot just between you and the small blind. So a raise here would have no steal potential (you cannot steal a sidepot that is empty), and your hand is not nearly strong enough to raise for value.

Action: You call. (There are three players and t2,550 in the pot.)

Flop: 8♠7♣2♥
Action: The small blind checks.

Question: Check or bet?
> **Answer:** Check. With your open-ended straight flush draw (and possible pair outs), you are the favorite to have the best hand at showdown. Were it not for the already-all-in player, you should absolutely bet. If your opponent called, he would

be doing so as an underdog. If he folded, you would win a big pot right now.

But the presence of the all-in player changes things. Say, for instance, the small blind is holding Q♥J♠ and you bet t1,200. He will probably fold due to bubble passivity and his weak hand. If you complete your uber-draw, then you cannot win any more money from the player who has folded (who may have paired an overcard and called a bet), so all you have done is limited your earnings potential.

Now suppose you miss your draw. Then your opponent will almost certainly take the pot against your 9-high, while meanwhile, the player you forced out could well have won with a paired overcard or even queen-high, thereby knocking out the all-in player and raising everyone's equity, yours included.

So in this hand, check the flop behind, and only plan on betting if you make your hand.

Hand 3-20

Blinds: t200-t400, 5 players

Your hand: You (t5,100) have A♠4♠ in the big blind.
Action to you: All fold to the button who makes an all-in call for t250. The loose small blind (t3,900) min-raises to t800.

Question: Do you fold, call, or reraise?
 Answer: Call. Your are getting better than 3-to-1 with a suited ace, and your call closes the action. Stay in.

Action: You call. (There are three players, t750 in the main pot, and t1,100 in the side pot.)

Flop: A♣T♣4♥

Action: The small blind checks.

Question: What should you do?

    Answer: Bet t1,200. There are two key differences between the previous hand, where a check-down was appropriate, and this hand, where it would be a big mistake:

1.   Your hand is vulnerable. Whereas in the previous hand, further cards could only help, you must now worry about a ten (counterfeiting your two pair), club (making a possible flush), or face card (making a potential straight or better two pair). You want hands that may improve to pay for the draw, simply fold, or even reraise with a hand almost certainly inferior to your two-pair.

2.   There is a side-pot. And indeed, it now exceeds the main pot, standing at t1,100. So winning the pot right here is just fine. Contrast this to the previous scenario where the side-pot you would be betting into was empty. This is another key difference; even should the small blind fold and the all-in player take the pot hitting a miracle runner-runner draw, you would still win the t1,100 on the table.

3.   It is very unlikely that keeping the other guy in will be necessary to bust the short stack.

4.   The short stack is so low that even if he wins the main pot it shouldn't help him much.

One last note concerning this hand. The small blind's pre-flop raise, rather than a call after the button's all-in, already violated the idea of implicit collusion. Even when implicit collusion is clearly correct, you cannot expect your opponents to always play optimally and check down. Low-stakes players are particularly likely to randomly bluff at an empty sidepot, even if this bet knocks out a player who might otherwise win, and they have no real hand.

If implicit collusion is the obvious move and yet your opponent is betting anyway, you should be inclined to fold even a good hand against a solid, perceptive player. Such a player could only be betting for value. But against a weak player of limited knowledge, be less inclined to fold a hand that you would normally expect to be best.

Raising All-in Without All Your Chips

Many of the high-blind situations we are discussing involve pre-flop all-ins, but you should not actually be raising your entire stack each time. Rather, you should sometimes make a raise large enough that you are clearly pot-committed, yet appears like it could be for value. This is because such a raise helps disguise your true blind-stealing intentions, particularly when you are getting short-stacked and an all-in may be seen (correctly) as a desperation move.

If you are making a smaller raise purely to avoid the appearance of a desperate all-in, make sure it is large enough that your opponents will realize you are too pot-committed to be driven out via a reraise. Indeed, the raise should often be for all your stack excluding a small fraction.

Here are two examples of "non all-in pushes" you might make at various blinds and stacks.

1. **Blinds:** t200-t400; **Stack:** t1,400; **Raise:** t1,000.

2. **Blinds:** t300-t600; **Stack** t2,200; **Raise:** t1,500.

However, an example that fails is:

3. **Blinds:** t100-t200; **Stack:** t1,800; **Raise:** t800.

This latter raise is a poor one if you would call an all-in anyway because an opponent with a low pocket pair (for example) may push reasoning there is a slight chance you would fold for the remaining t1,000.

Remember, then, that if you have been pushing a lot, or need to attack the blinds when it is obvious you are desperate to make a move, you should occassionally mix up your play with such a "non all-in push."[8]

Hand 3-21

Blinds: t200-t400, 6 players

Your hand: You (t1,850) have J♠8♠ under the gun.

Question: Fold, push, or make a different raise?
    Answer: Raise t1,200. You must play this hand rather than get blinded out, and with a bet of t1,200, you are clearly pot-committing yourself. But this variation on the all-in has two advantages:

1. It gives the image of a standard 3BB value raise rather than the desperate attempt to avoid getting blinded out that it actually is.

2. Psychologically, it is more intimidating that you have more chips (even a negligible quantity) in front of you. With an all-in, a player may simply click "Call" and be done with the

---

[8] There are a few situations where such a raise is indicated because you just might not call a reraise. These occur in endgame scenarios where saving a few chips may get you into the money.

decision-making process. When you have anything left, it suggests to opponents that there will be future decision-making involved in this hand, which many players would rather avoid.

Exploiting Pre-Flop Passivity as the Big Blind

Suppose you are the big blind, and all fold to the small blind, who limps. If you have yet to raise a hand he has limped, you should take his passive play literally. He most likely does not have a hand, and you are not being trapped. This is because he has no reason to assume you will raise. If the blinds are significant, i.e., one of you has 10BB or less, you should consider pushing any two cards.

Hand 3-22

Blinds: t200-t400, 6 players

Your hand: You (t2,000) have T♣8♠ in the big blind.
Action to you: All fold to the small blind (t2,500), with whom you have played no heads-up pots, who calls.

Question: Check or raise?
   Answer: Raise all-in. There is t800 on the table, a huge fraction of your t2,000 stack. The odds of you getting called are slim, and taking the pot now adds significantly to your winning chances. Lastly, even if you are called, you will still win on average at least 33 percent of the time unless you are facing a rare overpair.

Hand 3-23

Blinds: t400-t800, 3 players

Your hand: You (t4,200) have J♠9♠ in the big blind.

Action to you: The loose-passive button (t8,000) calls, and the TAG small blind (t6,600) completes.

Question: Check or raise?

    Answer: Raise all-in. You are getting short-stacked at these huge blinds, there is t2,400 on the table, nobody has shown real strength, and your mid-high suited semi-connectors play well against a variety of hands.

Calling All-ins and Profitable "Passive" Plays

Calling Short-Stacked All-ins as the Big Blind

So far in our high-blind section we have discussed almost exclusively aggressive principles — all-in re-steals, pushing with marginal hands when in danger of blinding out, coming over the top of high-blind limpers, and so forth. These are the tools you will need to thrive in high-blind sit 'n go play.

But as the blinds rise and short-stacks make desperation pushes, there can be many profitable calling opportunities. Indeed, many players with even loose styles will fold too frequently to such short-stack pushes.

Without further ado, the fundamental rule of high-blind pre-flop all-in calling:

> If you are getting better than 2-to-1 on a pre-flop all-in call, and your call closes the action, calling is nearly always correct.

The basis of this observation is that the most common worst-case scenario when calling is facing two overcards, in which case you are a 2-to-1 underdog. Those occasions when your opponent has an overpair are roughly balanced by those situations when your opponent is bluffing, and you are only a slight underdog or small favorite. So when getting better than 2-to-1 on a pre-flop heads-up all-in call, calling is higher cEV than folding.

This does not mean you should always call in such a situation. If, for instance, you are getting 11-to-5 pot odds with

168

two offsuit low cards and a call and loss will cripple you, you might consider folding. What it does mean, however, is that when getting better than 2-to-1, you need a reason *not* to call rather than a reason *to* call.

In the following examples, we consider calling all-ins in such borderline situations, or when you are getting worse than 2-to-1 but have a reasonable holding. You must weigh both the odds you are being offered for such a call, as well as the effects of a winning/losing call on your equity.

Hand 3-24

Blinds: t200-t400, 6 players

Your hand: You (t2,750) are the big blind with 7♣2♠.
Action to you: All fold to the LAG button (t850) who pushes. The small blind folds.

Question: Call or fold?
 Answer: Call. The button is liable to push here with almost any hand given his tiny stack. Risking t450 getting 3.5-to-1 against a random holding means folding is a huge mistake. You also have the potential to knock out an opponent who would otherwise be in contention if you fold. (As a side-note, 7♣2♠ is a 7-high hand and is only the worst possible hand in a multi-way pot. Heads-up, trey-deuce offsuit claims that dubious honor, and your 7♣ may actually come in handy against a low pocket pair or low suited ace.)

Hand 3-25

Blinds: t300-t600, 4 players

Your hand: You (t6,800) have 9♠7♣ in the big blind.

Action to you: The cutoff and button fold to the small blind (t1,566) who raises all-in.

Question: Call or fold?

> **Answer:** Call. This is a pot odds question. The pot is around t2,500, it costs around t1,200 to call, and so you are getting about 2-to-1. Remember, when you are getting 2-to-1, you need a reason *not* to call a small pre-flop all-in. Losing the t1,300 will not significantly affect your winning chances. The small blind is desperate and could be pushing any two cards. In this situation, you would only consider folding two unsuited low cards, and your mid offsuit semi-connectors are indeed good enough for a call.

Hand 3-26

Blinds: t300-t600, 6 players

Your hand: You (t2,400) have 6♥3♠ in the big blind. The table has become passive with most raises taking the blinds uncontested.

Action to you: UTG folds. The tight-passive UTG+1 (t1,900) raises all-in. Everyone folds to you in the big blind.

Question: Call or fold?

> **Answer:** Fold. You are indeed getting slightly better than 2-to-1. But here, you do have a reason not to call. Your hand is two offsuit low cards. If you call and lose, you fall to t1,100 (before posting your small blind, in fact), requiring a lucky run of cards to avoid elimination. If you fold, you still have blind-stealing power with a stack of 4BB.

One key to this hand is the "passive table" clause. It is important to recognize situations when no one is calling big raises before the money. You are a powerful contender with t2,400 when the blinds are t300-t600 and nobody wants to gamble. Take advantage of these promising table conditions by declining a marginal cEV call here, and be the subsequent aggressor nobody wants to call instead. Put another way, it is mathematically correct to pass up slightly positive EV gambles if a loss means that you won't be able to make better bets later.

Calling Large Pre-flop All-ins

Calling a significant all-in bet can pose certain benefits:

- **Value:** If the pot is offering odds that make calling positive cEV, then you can call for value.

- **Image:** This is particularly beneficial if you are calling a bet as the big blind. You want other players to fear aggressing on your blind, and calling an all-in is the best way to achieve this.

- **Knocking out a player.** This occurs when your marginal call forces a good player to gamble for all his chips. His potential elimination gives you, and everyone else at the table, added equity.

Your stack size relative to the bettor's is crucial. If you have him significantly out-chipped, then you should seize even slight expected edges. For example, suppose you have

in the big blind and put your opponent on two high cards. If the pot was laying any better than 2-to-1, you should call with even this trash hand. This is because calling benefits you in all three of the above regards.

Hand 3-27

Blinds: t300-t600, 5 players

Your hand: You (t5,500) have 7♠5♠ in the big blind.
Action to you: The aggressive UTG (t2,100) raises all-in. Everyone folds to you.

Question: Fold or call?

    Answer: Call. There is t3,000 in the pot, and the price of calling is t1,500. So you are getting a full 2-to-1 on your call. Against your opponent's most probable holding, two unpaired high cards, you are a 3-to-2 underdog. It is only against an unlikely overpair (aces down through fives) that you will be a heavy dog (at most 4-to-1), but these hands are much fewer than high card hands.

    Furthermore, you will sometimes be up against only one high card (such as A♣3♥), making you a mere 11-to-9 underdog. On balance, this is a call that will win chips, and as you can lose t1,500 without significantly affecting your winning chances, and your opponents will see you calling a t1,500 raise with 7-high to defend your blind, you should certainly call.

Remember: If you are getting 2-to-1 or better on a call, you need a reason *not* to call.

Hand 3-28

Blinds: t200-t400, 7 players

Your hand: You (t1,580) have 8♥8♦ on the button.
Action to you: Everyone folds to the hijack (t1,800) who raises all-in. The cutoff folds.

Question: Fold or call?
  Answer: Call. With 4BB in chips, you are looking to make a move. You probably have the best hand as an 11-to-9 favorite against two overcards, or 7-to-3 against one high card. Furthermore, with t600 in pseudo-dead money from the blinds, you stand to recover nearly 7-to-5 (t2,180-to-t1,580) on your investment. While you would rather be the aggressor yourself, the high blinds and strength of your hand make this a must-gamble situation.

Earlier we discussed distinguishing probable value raises from blind-steals. This skill is critical for assessing the risk of getting called on a re-steal, but it is useful in other contexts as well. The following is an application, and could be cross-referenced under the "Bubble" heading.

Hand 3-29

Blinds: t400-t800, 4 players

Your hand: You (t9,750) have K♠9♣ in the big blind.

Action to you: The experienced TAG sitting UTG (t2,900) raises all-in. The button (t1,900) and small blind (t4,600) fold.

Question: Fold or call?

> **Answer:** Call. This is, above all, a matter of pot odds. The pot is t4,100, and it costs you t2,300 to call: you are getting between 3-to-2 and 2-to-1 but a bit less ICM speaking. In this situation a good player will push many hands to avoid getting blinded out. He could easily be pushing any face card, suited connectors, a low pocket pair, etc. On balance, you should be about even money to take this pot.

Meanwhile, you are getting good odds, and a loss will still leave you in fine position as chip leader. In addition, you have the opportunity to knock out a dangerous player, and your opponents will see you making a big call with king-high.

Hand 3-30

Blinds: t200-t400, 9 players

Your hand: You (t1,260) have A♦9♦ in the cut-off.

Action to you: All fold to MP3 (t2,300) who raises all-in.

Question: Fold or call?

> **Answer:** Call. You have several hands to make a move before getting blinded out; you cannot let go of a hand as strong as A♦9♦, particularly with these decent odds (3-to-2), even if you must be the caller rather than the aggressor.

There is one more noteable context in which calling a bet is desirable. And this is when you are "Playing the Minuscule Stack."

Playing the Minuscule Stack (2BB or Fewer)

It is a generally held belief that the best strategy for short-stacked play is to pick a spot and push all-in to steal the blinds. This is typically the right idea. But depending on just how short-stacked you are, this principle may not hold.

Suppose you are on the losing end of a big coin-flip all-in and find yourself with under two big blinds left in chips. Clearly you will need to catch some hands and a little luck. But is there anything you can do to maximize your chances of a successful recovery?

The answer is yes. You must seize all opportunities to take advantage of pseudo-dead money. "Pseudo-dead money" refers to chips from players who will *probably* not be active in the pot. In particular this means blinds who must call an all-in or other large bet.

This leads to our primary observation:

> If your stack is two big blinds or fewer, and you are not a blind yourself, the Aggression Principle breaks down: you now want to be the one calling the bet. Indeed, certain situations require a stronger hand to make an all-in bet rather than to call one.

This is because when you are very short-stacked and are calling an all-in, the pseudo-dead money from the blinds is enormous relative to your stack.

To be concrete, suppose you have under 2BB, are not a blind yourself, and call an all-in from a late position bettor who has a stack of at least 3.5BB (preferably more). The blinds will usually fold to this all-in. When this happens and you win, you gain 2BB from the pusher plus another 1½ BB from the blinds, thereby increasing your stack by nearly a factor of 3. To reiterate: by calling you have the opportunity to triple up (more or less), while gambling against a single opponent.

You are looking for a situation where:

1. You believe the bettor is trying to steal the blinds (so you will not be faced with a premium hand when you call), and

2. It is likely that the bettor would succeed in stealing if you folded (i.e., because the blinds must call a large bet if they refuse to fold).

Then you will be taking a necessary gamble with a large amount of pseudo-dead money in the pot relative to your stack.

Furthermore, when the blinds are big, it does not take a monster hand to blind-steal. You will often be up against two medium-high cards, such as

or a low pocket pair. Few cards are significant underdogs to these hands.

Playing the super-short stack requires keen intuition and a willingness to take advantage of any opportunity that may present itself. Calling a blind-stealing bet with the prospect of tripling up against a single opponent is often the best such opportunity you will come across.

Now suppose you have a minuscule stack and are one of the blinds yourself, do you still want to be the one calling a large bet? The answer is yes. You are now forfeiting your expected take of either the big blind or the small blind, depending on which blind you are. However, since your posted blind will be significant relative to your stack, you will almost certainly want to gamble here with a call.

In the beginning of "Part Three: High-Blind Play," we stated that you never want to find yourself with under 3BB as this is a terrible situation where you are too weak even to blind-steal. But it can happen if you lose a race to a slightly smaller stack. While your equity does plummet in such situations, you can still make a solid run at returning to contention if you play smart and follow this advice, rather than blindly shoving your chips into the pot one or two hands after taking a bad beat.

Lastly, with a stack between 2 to 3BB, just look for a decent hand to play, whether you are the bettor or the raiser.

Hand 3-31

Blinds: t200-t400, 8 players

Your hand: You (t535) have T♥2♠ in the big blind.
Action to you: All fold to the loose-aggressive button (t1,800) who raises all-in. The small blind folds.

Question: What is your move?
Answer: Call. The bet is equivalent to an all-in of t935. So the question is whether you want to pay your last t535 to enter a t1,535 pot with a trash hand. The answer is yes. If you fold, you have a pitiful t535 and need an incredible run of cards to survive. So getting nearly 3-to-1 pot odds, gamble here as a probable 2-to-1 or better underdog (as your opponent's likely worst case holding is two overcards). If you win, you have over t2,000 and are solidly back in contention. If you lose, you are forfeiting little equity, as you would otherwise be playing with a stack of just over 1BB.

Hand 3-32

Blinds: t200-t400, 8 players

Your hand: You (t750) are on the button with J♠9♣.
Action to you: Everyone folds to the tight-aggressive cut-off (t2,000) who pushes all-in. The blinds both have significant stacks.

Question: Call or fold?
> **Answer:** Call. This is a perfect minuscule-stack calling situation. Your stack is under 2 big blinds, you are up against a near-certain blind steal, the blinds will most likely fold against this large bet, and your hand is reasonable. What a perfect time to gamble. If you win, you will have tripled up and are right back in contention. Folding will indeed keep you alive now, but with under 2 big blinds left, you will need incredible luck to avoid getting blinded out. Rather than passively fold and hope for the best, seize this opportunity and gamble! You will probably be about a 3-to-2 underdog against a hand such as Q♦8♥ or A♠2♠. If you do win this positive cEV gamble, then your stack is over t2,000 again.

Hand 3-30

Blinds: t300-t600, 4 players

Your hand: You (t1,500) have J♣T♠ on the button. Both blinds are large-stacked.
Action to you: The tight-aggressive UTG (t2,500) raises all-in.

Question: Call or fold?
> **Answer:** Call. Your opponent would probably push with any non-trash hand in this situation, as he should to avoid getting

blinded out. You may even be the favorite with a jack high, and if not, it is very unlikely you will be worse than a 3-to-2 underdog. It is also unlikely one of the blinds will call a 4BB+ raise with a caller. If you win, you will have t3,900, the cutoff will be crippled, and you will be right back in contention. This is too great a possible reward to pass up.

Many players fold here wanting only to maximize their chances of moneying. But notice two things:

1. The most likely outcome if you fold is the blinds folding behind you, in which case you figure to be blinded out in two hands.

2. Even if one of the blinds both calls *and* wins, while you would be in the money, your chances of placing better than third are very low.

Hand 3-34

Blinds: t300-t600, 6 players

Your hand: You (t1,080) have A♠2♠ UTG+1.
Action to you: UTG folds.

Question: What is your play?
  Answer: Push. With under 2BB you cannot expect to execute a successful blind-steal. But with a robust hand such as A♠2♠, you simply cannot fold waiting for a better opportunity. Even against a premium hand such as A♦K♣ or K♥K♣, you will not be much worse than a 2-to-1 underdog. Calling an all-in with your minsicule stack would be best, but that does not mean you should not push yourself if you wake up with a good hand.

Here is an example where your blind pot-commits you with your minsicule stack, and so your best option is a stop n' go.

Hand 3-35

Blinds: t200-t400, 7 players

Your hand: You (t688) have T♠3♣ in the big blind.
Action to you: All fold to the loose-passive cutoff (t2,000), who calls. The button and small blind fold.

Question: Check or raise?
> **Answer:** Check. The pot has t1,000, more than your stack, and you are desperate to make a move. But there is effectively no chance another t688 will get your loose-passive opponent to leave the pot before the flop. So check with the intention of betting your remaining chips after the flop.

Action: You check. (There are two players and t1,000 in the pot.)

Flop: J♠4♣4♦

Question: Check or bet?
> **Answer:** Bet t500. If he has even an ace-high, expect to be called. But if he has two random high cards, your seemingly confident bet may move him off the hand, and if not, you will still usually win if you spike a ten or trey as you will a full quarter of the time.

Hand 3-36

Blinds: t200-t400

Your hand: You (t585) have 9♦6♦ in the small blind. The big blind has t2,800.

Action to you: Everyone folds.

Question: What is your move?

> **Answer:** Call. The combination of your posted t200 small blind and marginal hand force you to play. But if you simply shove in the remainder of you chips, it will be only another t385 for the big blind to call, which he figures to do with any two cards. But if you just call and he checks, there is a chance he will fold to your (automatic) t385 bet if the flop misses him entirely.

In cases such as these, thinking logically about your different options will increase your chances of winning a pot you might otherwise have no shot at — a solid technique to improve your long-term earnings.

When You Should *Not* Attack High-Blind Passivity

We have made it a theme that you should relentlessly attack high-blind pre-flop passivity namely by making big steal raises against loose-passive high-blind limpers or min-raisers when the combination of the blinds and the bet(s) are significant relative to your stack ... and you have at least a decent hand. But this principle can break down when your passive opponent meets two criteria:

1. He is a very loose caller.

2. He has a much larger stack than yours.

This type of hyper-loose big-stacked opponent is liable to call just for the sake of calling when your stack is comparatively small. He is found most often in lower-stakes sit 'n go's and you should only go up against him for value since he folds so rarely. If you believe you are up against such an opponent, and his stack is much larger than yours, you may be better off waiting for a better opportunity unless your hand is well above-average.

Hand 3-37

Blinds: t200-t400, 7 players

Your hand: You (t1,600) have J♣T♠ in the big blind.
Action to you: Pre-flop: All fold to the extremely loose-passive button (t5,700), who limps. You have seen this player call a large all-in reraise with A♥4♦ after HBLing during a t100-t200 hand. The small blind folds.

Question: Check or raise?
  Answer: Check. There is t1,000 on the table (nearly two-thirds your stack), nobody has shown strength, and you have a reasonable hand. So why not push? Because this type of opponent will probably call another t1,200 with any two cards he was willing to limp with. His hand will probably be a slight favorite to your jack-high, so by pushing all-in, you are effectively agreeing to gamble for your tournament life against a better hand. Instead, take the free flop, and continue if you catch almost any piece of it.

Action: You check. (There are two players and t1,000 in the pot.)

Flop: 4♣2♠2♥

Question: Check or bet?

> **Answer:** Check. Unless your opponent has a pair, this flop missed him completely. But do not bluff. Just as before, he is loose and big-stacked, and is likely to call a bet with two random overcards. Your gameplan is to check/fold unless he allows a free ten or jack to hit, in which case you should bet out and expect to get called by a worse hand.

Hand 3-38

Blinds: t200-t400, 7 players

Your hand: You (t1,450) are the small blind with K♠6♣.

Action to you: All fold to the loose-passive cut-off (t3,500) who min-raises to t800. The button folds.

Question: What is your move?

> **Answer:** Fold. With just over 3BB in chips and 6 opponents left, you are happy to risk all your chips making an aggressive play. But this is not the time to do it. There are three reasons:

1. Your hand is very marginal. You are ahead of a minority of your opponent's possible holdings (queen-jack, jack-ten suited, or a stone bluff come to mind).

2. Your opponent will not fold. Your bet will be t1,450 + t200 = t1,650 total. Therefore, there will be t1,650 + t400 + t800 = t2,850 on the table, and it will be another t850 for him to call. Furthermore, he is right to call with any two cards in this situation, a fact he will recognize intuitively even if he is not explicitly calculating pot odds.

3. With over 3BB left, you are still in position to blind-steal if you fold.

Hand 3-39

Blinds: t300-t600, 6 players

Your hand: You (t2,100) have K♠Q♠ on the button.
Action to you: The super-loose chip leader (t6,800) min-raises to t1,200.

Question: What is your move?

Answer: Reraise all-in. Like the previous examples, you have no hope of getting your opponent to fold to your reraise. But your hand is strong enough that you figure to often be ahead, or at least a very small underdog. And a raise should at least force out the blinds, leaving a vast t900 on the table to sweeten the pot.

Hand 3-40

Blinds t200-t400, 8 players

Your hand: You (t1,700) have A♠6♣ on the button.
Action to you: All fold to the loose-passive cut-off (t4,000) who makes a characteristic min-raise.

Question: What is your move?

Answer: Fold. If you push, the cutoff will call. Even if he has no clue of pot odds (and therefore does not realize he is correct to call with any two cards for t900 on a t3,100 pot), he will intuitively realize he must call this small reraise, particularly since he is relatively large-stacked.

With a stack of 4BB in this situation, unless you have a solid hand (good enough to call with), look to steal rather than make a pot-committed opponent gamble with your marginal re-steal. This is because you still have stealing fold equity, and so unless you have a premium hand, you should wait to aggress against shorter stacks or tighter players. Such patience is rewarded in the form of a higher-percentage chance of winning the t800 in blind/ante money uncontested, i.e., you will have a strong chance of increasing your stack by 50 percent without even a showdown simply by waiting to attack in a better spot.

Short-Handed Play

Limp-Stealing From the Small Blind

We have stated that high-blind limping, due to its passivity, should be avoided as a general rule. But you should occasionally mix up your play by limping from the small blind against a non-aggressive big blind. This is typically done with a good or average hand as you normally fold a trash hand and raise a strong hand.

If you limp with a good-to-average hand and he raises, tend to fold. But if he checks, make a small bet (1 through 1.5 times the minimum) at the flop if you catch any piece or believe your opponent is likely to fold to a small bet. If you do check and he checks behind, you *must* make a small turn bet regardless of what hits.

Hand 3-41

Blinds: t400-t800, heads-up

Your hand: You (t8,100) have 7♠5♠ on the button. Your opponent is loose-passive.

Question: What is your play?
Answer: Call. With just over ten blinds, a loose-passive opponent, and a mid-card speculative hand, this is a good opportunity for the limp-steal.

Action: Your opponent checks. (There are two players and t1,600 in the pot.)

Flop: J♦4♥3♥

Action: He checks.

Question: Bet or check behind?
Answer: Min-bet t800. You are getting 2-to-1 on this investment, and if he has missed the flop, he will probably fold. If not, you may comfortably fold to a raise, and have a 4-out gutshot in case of a call (and hitting a five or seven may win as well).

Hand 3-42

Blinds: t300-t600, 5 players

Your hand: You (t6,100) have J♠4♠ in the small blind. The big blind (t3,000) is tight-passive.
Action to you: Everyone folds.

Question: What is your move?
Answer: Push! You are near the bubble against a single tight opponent, and your suited jack is not hopeless in the face of an unlikely call. This is not the time to limp-steal, and if you do, a good opponent will respond by pushing almost any two cards. Yet let us suppose ...

Action: You elect to call and the big blind checks. (There are two players and t1,200 in the pot.)

Flop: K♦4♥2♠

Question: Check or bet?
Answer: Bet t800. With mid pair and a backdoor flush draw, your hand is very likely best. So bet here expecting to take the pot immediately.

Action: You bet t800 and he raises t2,200.

Question: What do you do?

    Answer: Fold. With this pot-committing raise, he is telling you he is going to play the hand out. Therefore, his bet is effectively his full t3,000 stack meaning you are getting about 5-to-2 to take this hand to the showdown. However, you are almost certainly beat.

    Tight-passive players (like most others) will usually not make a pot-committing raise in the face of aggression without mid pair beat when it is right before the money. You are most likely up against a weak king, in which case you are worse than a 3-to-1 underdog to improve to the best hand. You made a low-risk attempt to take this pot, and it failed. Leave the hand, and continue to menace the table with your remaining t5,000.

3-Handed Play

    When the play gets down to 3-handed many players are so happy to be in the money that they reason as follows (at least subconsciously): "I have already made a profit in this tournament, so now is basically a freeroll. If I place any better, great. If I bust out here, hey — at least I'm still ahead."

    You must resist this reasoning at all costs. You are playing for long-term profit, not just to finish in-the-money in one particular tournament. Remember, you win considerably more with one first than two thirds.

    Your best approach now is standard high-blind aggression. Blind-steal and re-steal often, throwing in the occasional call from the small blind when the blinds are lower or the big blind has been passive.

Hand 3-43

Blinds: t200-t400, 3 players

Your hand: You (t5,800) have A♠2♠ on the button.

Question: What is your play?

    Answer: Raise to t1,000. You have what figures to be the best hand in 3-way play, so make a standard raise to take the blinds.

Hand 3-44

Blinds: t600-t1,200, 3 players

Your hand: You (t2,800) have K♠7♣ in the small blind.
Action to you: The button (t5,000) raises all-in.

Question: Call or fold?

    Answer: Call. You have a decent hand for high-blind 3-handed play. Gamble here with excellent odds (t4,600-to-t1,600, or nearly 3-to-1) rather than get blinded out.

Hand 3-45

Blinds: t400-t800, 3 players

Your hand: You (t8,000) have Q♠9♣ in the big blind.
Action to you: The loose-passive button (t7,600) calls. The small blind (t2,400) completes.

Question: Check or raise?

    Answer: Check. Raising all-in here is not unreasonable, but even if the button folds, the small blind may well seize the excellent pot odds and call with any hand he was willing to complete with.

Action: You check. (There are three players and t2,400 in the pot.)

Flop: T♥9♥2♥
Action: The small blind checks.

Question: Check or bet?
> **Answer:** Bet t1,500. Your mid pair figures to be best even with the hearts, and so you should bet out yourself rather than call a bet.

Action: You bet t1,500. The button calls. The small blind raises all-in for another t500.

Question: What is your move?
> **Answer:** Call. The pot is t7,400 and it costs you t500 to call. While you should be decidedly concerned by this action, you cannot fold getting nearly 15-to-1 with middle pair.

Action: You call, as does the button. (There are two players and t8,400 in the pot.)

Turn: A♥

Question: Check or bet?
> **Answer:** Check. Your hand is nearly worthless with this fourth heart and ace, so check and hope for a free showdown.

Action: You check, and the button pushes all-in for t4,800.

Question: Call or fold?
> **Answer:** Fold. At this point, you can beat no hand but a total bluff. You are only getting 5-to-2, and you have t5,200 remaining. Save it.

Action: You fold. The small blind shows J♠T♠, and the button flips Q♥J♦ for a winning flush.

Hand 3-46

Blinds: t100-t200, 3 players

Your hand: You (t4,800) have 7♦6♦, J♠5♣, or A♥7♣ on the button. The blinds (t8,300 and t6,300) seem tight, but you have seen both make the occasional re-steal.

Question: What is your play with each hand?

Answer: 7♦6♦. With a quality speculative hand and position, aggress to win immediately or play a disguised hand in position. Raise to t600, and if reraised, you have an easy fold.

J♠5♣. Fold this trash hand.

A♥7♣. While A♥7♣ is a stronger hand than 7♦6♦, it is also harder to play in this situation. I recommend a smaller bet. If you face a re-steal, you can fold with little impact. If you are called, you can still potentially get away if an ace hits and you feel you are out-kicked. So raise to t450 or so here.

Hand 3-47

Blinds: t300-t600, 3 players

Your hand: You (t11,000) have T♠8♠ in the big blind.

Action to you: The loose-passive button (t6,000) min-raises t1,200. The small blind (t2,100) folds.

Question: Do you fold, call, or raise?

Answer: Push all-in. Players tend to decline certain gambles for all their chips when a much shorter-stacked opponent is about to be blinded out in third or fourth place. So the button will need a solid hand to call. Furthermore, there is over t2,000 on the table, nobody has shown real strength (a min-raise does not qualify), you are not risking your own tournament life, and you are only a big underdog to eights through aces.

Your read on the button is important here. If he is a tricky tight-aggressive player whom you have never seen min-raise, fold. There is too high a chance he is trying to get action on a high pocket pair or two premium overcards. But for most players, a min-raise is not a show of genuine strength. It is a cheap attempt to pick up the blinds. If you move all-in over the min-raiser, and he is not priced in (usually requiring you to reraise at least 3 times his bet), he will most often fold.

Heads-Up

Many refer to online heads-up play as a "crapshoot," as the often-monstrous blinds may force opponents to prematurely butt heads with weak hands. To be sure, there is luck involved at this point. But the huge increase in payout for first place makes heads-up skill an essential component of your sit 'n go repertoire.

You should always play aggressively, but your specific strategy will depend on your opponent.

If he is passive, you want to call more often on the button, folding to most raises (which indicate genuine strength). If you miss the flop completely, min-bet often, particularly against tight-passive players who will often fold. Check/folding is usually the best line against calling stations when you miss.

If you hit any piece of the flop against your passive opponent, bet for value relentlessly. Furthermore, never leave the hand (where you have hit the flop) unless you are both non-pot committed and have strong indication that you are beaten, such as a reraise when you have bottom pair.

And if you are dealt an above-average starting hand, certainly raise pre-flop for value.

If your opponent is aggressive, the confrontation usually turns into a pushing war. In this case, push your stronger hands (see Appendix B: "Pushing Tables" starting on page 247 and look at those cases when you are small blind), and call/fold your weaker ones. The more liable he is to reraise a limp, the more you should fold hands too weak to push.

Against an opponent who is pushing very often, you should call with any hand that is clearly above-average, such as K♠8♣, 6♦6♣, Q♠J♠, or A♦3♣. This idea is consistent with the general theory of heads-up play:

> Always play aggressively, but exploit any weaknesses you have found in your individual opponent.

Note that weakness in this case does not necessarily mean passivity (although it often does). For example, if the blinds are t100-t200 and your opponent (t8,000) is pushing all-in with 90 percent of his hands, you (t12,000) should exploit this overbetting tendency via loosening up your calling range.

One final observation about heads-up. If a move is positive cEV, it is also positive equity. To see why, suppose you are playing a 10 player $109 sit 'n go with prizes of $500, $300, and $200. Then once you reach 2-man play, the situation is identical to one in which you and your opponent have each been awarded $300, as neither you nor him can do worse than place second, and you two are now playing a winner-take-all battle where the winner gets the remaining $200. So seize any edge in heads-up play.

Hand 3-48

Blinds: t200-t400, heads-up

Your hand: You (t2,600) have 2♠2♦ as the big blind. The button (t16,200), an extreme loose-aggressive player who has been pushing consistently since the start of t200-t400, raises all-in.

Question: Call or fold?

Answer: Call. The odds are about 15-to-1 against him having an overpair, and you are a slight favorite against most overcard hands. Furthermore, with your t400 blind sitting out there, you are getting better than even money odds. Lastly, with a short-stack and uber-aggressive opponent, you need to make a stack quick to avoid getting blinded out.

Hand 3-49

Blinds: t300-t600, heads-up

Your hand: You (t2,000) are in the big blind with J♠5♠.
Action to you: Your tight-aggressive opponent (t17,100) raises all-in.

Question: Call or fold?

Answer: Call. You are in an unfortunate situation, but calling is the superior option. There is t3,200 on the table, and it costs you t2,000 to call. Your opponent will push with many hands here, and if you fold, you are left with under three blinds after posting next hand. So getting over 3-to-2, gamble here with your average hand and hope for the best.

Hand 3-50

Blinds: t600-t1,200, heads-up

Your hand: You (t5,000) have J♠2♠ on the button.

Question: What is your move?

> **Answer:** Raise all-in. *It is a much bigger mistake to allow yourself to get blinded out in high-blind play than it is to make a marginal push.* Here there is t1,800 on the table from the blinds alone, and you have an average heads-up hand in case of a call. Be the aggressor in heads-up high-blind play!

Hand 3-51

Blinds: t300-t600, heads-up

Your hand: You (t9,400) have 7♠5♠ on the button. Your opponent (t9,700) is tight-aggressive.

Question: What is your move?

> **Answer:** Limp from the small blind with your quality speculative hand and position.

Action: You call for another t300 and your opponent checks. (There are two players and t1,200 in the pot.)

Flop: A♠K♥K♠
Action: He min-bets t600.

Question: What is your move?

> **Answer:** Raise to t1,400. It is very unlikely your opponent has any piece of this flop as he did not raise pre-flop. Even if he was holding onto an ace or king, it is much more likely he would check to you (the likely bettor), rather than lead right out with a bet. Most likely, your opponent realizes the flop is unlikely to have helped you and wants to steal the pot right here with a small bet. If your raise does not induce an immediate fold, you are done putting chips in this pot unless you hit your flush.

Hand 3-52

Blinds: t400-t800, heads-up

Your hand: You (t6,000) have 9♥4♠ on the button. Your opponent is aggressive.

Question: What is your move?
> **Answer:** Fold. You want to be the aggressor in high-blind heads-up, but do not blindly push trash hands.

Hand 3-53

Blinds: t400-t800, heads-up

Your hand: You (t9,200) have A♠4♠ in the big blind.
Action to you: Your opponent (t9,600) raises to t1,600.

Question: What is your move?
> **Answer:** Reraise all-in. There is already t2,400 on the table, and your suited ace is a monster heads-up. Unless your opponent's raise is uncharacteristic (such as from a TAG who is always pushing or folding), it is unlikely to indicate genuine strength. Even if he is slowplaying a monster hand, you cannot be much worse than a 2-to-1 underdog unless he has exactly two aces.

Hand 3-54

Blinds: t300-t600, heads-up

Your hand: You (t11,000) have K♠2♠ on the button.

Question: What is your move?

    Answer: Raise to t1,500. You do not want to push with this decent hand against your opponent's 15-odd BB. It is also too strong to fold. Raising to 2.5BB will often win the pot pre-flop. If not, you can safely fold to a reraise, and generally make a standard continuation bet at the flop if called.

Hand 3-55

Blinds: t200-t400, heads-up

Your hand: You (t9,100) have 5♥2♥ in the big blind.
Action to you: Your opponent calls.

Question: Check or raise?

    Answer: Check. Your stacks are large relative to the blinds, and you have a weak hand out of position. Take a free flop.

Action: You check. (There are two players and t800 in the pot.)

Flop: J♥9♣3♥

Question: Check or bet?

    Answer: Check. If he checks behind, you get a free card to draw to your low flush. If he bets, then …

Action: You check, and he min-bets t400.

Question: What is your play?

    Answer: Raise to t1,000. This is a semi-bluff. Heads-up, there is a strong chance he missed the flop and will now fold. If he calls, you may still hit your flush and win a big pot. And if he reraises, tend to leave the hand (barring a small reraise), knowing you are beat at the time.

Action: You raise to t1,000 and he calls. (There are two players and t2,800 in the pot)

Turn: 6♦

Question: Check or bet?
 Answer: Bet around one-half the pot, say $1,400. You now have a gutshot straight draw to accompany your flush draw, giving you 12 outs to improve to a monster hand head's up. Since you would therefore have the odds to call a reasonable bet if you checked and he bet, you are probably better off betting yourself. This is particularly true as your opponent has shown little strength so far, and betting out gives you added fold equity while still allowing you to save your remaining chips if he comes over top with a big reraise. In addition, if he smooth-calls with a strong hand (intending to trap you), you will often stack him if you make your hand on the river.

Hand 3-56

Blinds: t100-t200, heads-up

Your hand: You (t10,000) have 2♠2♣ on the button. Your opponent (t9,700) is on the tight side.

Question: Fold, call, or raise?
 Answer: Raise t600. You have a low pocket pair in position, so raise to win immediately or play a bigger pot in position.

Action: You raise to t600 and he calls. (There are two players and t1,200 in the pot.)

Flop: J♥5♦4♠
Action: He checks.

Question: Check or bet?

> **Answer:** Bet t750. It is likely your underpair is best, and if your opponent did not catch a piece of this flop, he will probably fold against your pre-flop and flop shows of strength.

Action: You bet t750 and he min-raises t1,500.

Question: Fold, call, or raise?

> **Answer:** Fold. Your opponent's pre-flop smooth-call and flop check-raise indicate great strength, particularly in light of your aggressive actions. He almost certainly has a pair of deuces beat, and if so, you are only 5 percent to improve on the next card (and could, conceivably, be drawing dead against a made set). Fold now and cut your losses.

Hand 3-57

Blinds: t100-t200, heads-up

Your hand: You (t7,500) have XY on the button. Your opponent (t12,300) is an average player, quite capable of playing a hand, but slightly passive.

Question: How you play this hand depends on XY. So let us see how you might play various hands in this low-blind heads-up button situation.

> **Answer:** Q♠2♥. Call. A weak queen-high is an average, or slightly above average, hand heads-up. Plus you have position, and so you should play. One high card, one low card hands tend not be real money-makers though, so I would either just call or perhaps make a small raise to around t450.

> 6♠5♠. Raise to t600. Mid suited connectors are a fine holding heads-up with position. Your hand can hit the flop in

many ways, and *hitting the flop at all usually gives you the best hand heads-up*. Furthermore, since you have both shown aggression and camoflaged your hand (a larger raise usually indicates something besides a 6-high), *your decisions in the hand subsequent to your initial raise will generally be easier.*

For example ... He comes over the top of you before the flop, or the flop comes three overcards and he bets out — then you can easily get away from the hand. If you flop either nothing or a weak piece of the flop (such as a flop of K♥Q♥5♥), then you make a standard one-third to one-half pot continuation bet. This will often take the pot immediately. And since you have indicated strength pre- and post-flop, and a flop came that looks like it might easily have hit you, you can again slip away quickly against a near-certain better hand if you are played back at.

As a result of this easier decision-making: *You have the potential to win a large or small pot from your opponent, whereas your opponent only has potential to win a small pot from you.* This is because your opponent will put you on a different hand than you actually have, namely high cards or possibly a pair. So if he is betting or putting up any resistance, then you fold unless you have a monster. Meanwhile, hands like 6♠5♠ are quality speculative hands, so you have the potential to flop disguised gold and double up if he catches a piece. For instance, your opponent has K♣T♥ and the flop comes T♦6♥5♣ — he will get it all-in with you at the flop. Or the flop comes 7♠4♣3♣, he checks and you check behind. The turn comes the T♥, he bets out, you come over him for a small raise, and by the river your value betting wins you a huge pot.

6♥3♦. Fold. This is a trash hand. If your opponent is extremely passive, calling with any two may be positive cEV, in which case you could call. But realize the hand has no present strength and almost zero post-flop potential.

Q♥T♣. Raise to t500. This is a solid hand heads-up, and come in for a standard raise. Winning before the flop is great, but Q♥T♣ also plays well post-flop, especially in position.

Hand 3-58

Blinds: t100-t200, heads-up

Your hand: You (t7,500) have K♠3♣ on the button. Your opponent (t12,300) is an average player.

Question: What is your move?

Answer: Call. You have position and an above-average hand heads-up, so folding is not an option. However, a weak king-high is a hand that lends itself to small pots for the reasons discussed above. If your opponent is capable of folding to small raises, you might raise to $450 or so. But rarely is it to your advantage to create a large pot when playing an X-low hand (X = A, K, Q, or J). This is because your pre-flop show of strength will make your opponent weary when the X card hits, and so for him to play a big pot, he will often have you beat (with bottom two pair, for example)

Hand 3-59

Blinds: t400-t800, heads-up

Your hand: You (t6,300) have K♠8♣ in the big blind. Your multi-tabling TAG opponent has pushed the last five hands on the button.

Action to you: He raises all-in from the button.

Question: Call or fold?

    Answer: Call. The pot is t800 (your blind) + t7,100 (the portion of his stack matching your blind and the remainder of your stack) = t7,900. Meanwhile, it costs you t6,300 to call, so you are only getting about 5-to-4. But despite these marginal pot odds, the action indicates your opponent is most likely pushing any non-trash hand, and a decent king is well above average.

    Against an aggressive opponent like this, eventually all your chips are going into the center before the flop. Despite being the caller, you should do this now while you have a decent hand and the blinds have yet to cripple you. (If you walk away from this hand and the next three, for instance, you will be down to a mere t3,900.)

    Note that your opponent's recklessly aggressive style is not so bad a strategy for high-blind heads-up play, and is indeed much better than folding all but a good hand.

Stack-Dependent Strategy on the Bubble

Your strategy when 4- or 5-handed should almost always be classified as "aggressive." However, let us be more specific as to optimal strategy for players of different stack sizes when approaching the money. To be concrete, suppose the blinds are t100-t200 and there are four players left:

Player A	t8,000
Player B	t3,500
Player C	t1,100
Player D	t400

What game plan should you choose as chip leader, average stack, short stack, and minuscule stack?

Player A's Game Plan

If you are player A, you should be very aggressive. If you are the opener and D is not in the big blind, then you raise t400 to t500 with any non-trash hand. Expect everyone to fold a significant majority of the time. If you are called by B, tend to make a continuation bet of t500 or so regardless of the flop. If he bets first, or reraises your pre-flop or flop bets, it is very likely you are beaten unless you hold a premium hand since he will avoid taking a serious chance of elimination when he can coast into the money.

If you are called/reraised by C or D, then going to the showdown as an underdog is not so bad. You may win by outdrawing, and if you lose, you are still a monster chip leader with t7,600 or t6,900. Prolonging the bubble may even be beneficial if the blinds will rise soon and your opponents exhibit standard bubble risk aversion.

Now let us suppose another player has entered the pot before you. When that player is C or D, you have largely a pot odds value decision on your hand. See the sections on calling all-in bets for more on this topic. More interesting is when B enters the pot before you. Unless he makes a pot-committing raise pre-flop, you should reraise (or at least call) his bet, almost independent of your holding (unless he is aware of that strategy and is thus often trapping.)

For example suppose B is an aggressive player under-the-gun. You (A) are on the button with

D is the small blind. C is the big blind.

B min-raises to t400. You should reraise to t1,200 to t1,400. The blinds will fold most hands hoping that the two big stacks collide, and B will usually only continue if he has a premium hand with the presence of the minuscule and short stacks. So your reraise will usually win the t700 on the table immediately.

If B reraises you all-in, be confident he has a monster, and tend to fold despite the excellent pot odds as you will usually be gambling against an overpair. If B smooth-calls your reraise, be suspicious, and tend not to invest more chips in the pot unless he shows weakness by checking to you twice[9] (in which case bet one-third to one-half the pot), or you connect solidly with the flop.

---

[9] And even this could be a trap.

Lastly, let us consider when all have folded to you in the small blind. Against player D, assuming he will call with any two, then you must pay t300 for a t500 pot and should therefore min-raise him all-in with almost any two cards getting such favorable odds with no risk to your chip position.

Against player C, you should shove any two cards as he will need a real hand to call with Player D about to be blinded out. And even if he does call, you are only risking t1,100 of your t8,000 (in chips).

Against player B, raise any decent hand to t600 to t800, and call with the remainder of your hands (no matter how weak). The raise will win outright unless B has a monster hand, so even getting 1-to-2 on your steal investment (assuming a raise to t700), this will show long-run chip profit since B will fold more than 2 times in 3. Meanwhile, if he calls, you may still hit the flop.

Even if your hand is two low offsuit cards, and you are out of position, getting 3-to-1 on your call is worth it against the vast majority of players since they will frequently check behind and then fold to a small continuation bet (of t200 to t300) unless they have a very solid pre-flop hand or connect solidly with the flop.

In summary, as bubble chip leader, Player A must accumulate even more chips. This is done through ruthless aggression as well as value calls when the short or minuscule stack pushes and you have a chip advantage.

Player B's Game Plan

When it comes to attacking C and D, or calling all-ins from these shorter-stacked players, your strategy should be comparable to A's. Even if you lose an all-in against C, you will still be second in chips with t2,400 during the t100-t200 level with the minuscule-stacked D about to be blinded out.

The significant question is how you should deal with Player A. The problem is similar to the introductory example in the "Bubble Play" sub-chapter starting on page 147 in "Part Three:

High-Blind Play." You can only find yourself in a positive equity pre-flop gamble for all your chips against Player A if you have precisely aces or kings. If A realizes this and/or is re-stealing liberally, then you should steal very rarely when A is yet to act. If A is tight-passive and/or unaware, then aggress on him with your better hands — just be willing to leave the hand if he plays back and you do not have a monster hand.

An interesting A-B dynamic occurs when A has already entered the pot, and you are considering re-stealing, or even calling. If you have a hand that figures to be considerably ahead of A's pushing range, simply reraise all-in so as to maximize your fold equity (since you want to avoid gambling in this spot to the greatest extent possible). If you are unsure about whether to contest A's aggression with a big re-steal, fold as a default.

Should you sometimes smooth-call a raise by A? Yes. A good calling opportunity would be in a situation as follows:

A, playing aggressively, makes a standard raise to t500 from under-the-gun. You (Player B) are on the button with A♠K♣. C and D are in the blinds.

Here you should call. This is by process of elimination. Your hand/position combination are too strong to fold.

Reraising would be reasonable with many stack sizes, but your stack size is rather awkward. If you reraise to t1,500 or so, you will be put in a terrible situation if A goes all-in. (The correct play would be a crying fold.) And if you reraise all-in, you do not want a call with your two unpaired high cards as getting called without aces or kings decreases your equity, and so your primary motive in reraising must be to steal. Risking t3,500 to win t800 is marginal, particularly if A is loose and will call with some weaker holdings.

But calling works well here. Most of the time both blinds will fold. If you hit an ace or a king, play very fast at the flop, and otherwise check/fold. You want to minimize your chip swings at all costs with these stack sizes, and smooth-calling with your ace-king in position is the best way to accomplish this task.

In summary, Player B should play similarly to Player A when contending with Players C and D. He should avoid most pots against A, and those he does play, he must either keep small or have an overwhelming edge.

Player C's Game Plan

Most players in C's position go into "shutdown" mode. They reason that since D is going to be blinded out soon, they should take few — if any — risks to ensure moneying. The problem with this reasoning is that many times, what seems a done deal (such as D bubbling out) can change drastically in only a few hands.

For instance, suppose C shuts down for two orbits, while meanwhile, D doubles up (and gets the pseudo-dead blind money) by calling a 3BB raise on the button with

and then successfully blind-steals once the subsequent orbit.

Situations like the above occur routinely. In this case, C will have essentially switched places with D, with new stacks of t500 and t1,100, respectively. And it is now C who will most often bubble out.

So when you are Player C in this scenario, do not look to force a play, but maintain your aggression and still push decent hands into tight players. Most important: Do not allow yourself to get blinded out. The Fundamental Theorem of High-Blind Sit 'n Go Play still applies when there is a very small stack. You just have to choose your spots carefully.

So suppose you (Player C) are under-the-gun with

A is the button and has been passive. B is the small blind and has been playing few hands recently. And D is the big blind with t200 after posting.

You should push. You have a stack of 5.5BB, you have a very strong hand for high-blind 4-way play, and the presence of a player who may be blinded out soon should not change your decision.

Also, if you fold here, D may well win the pot, in which case a mere three hands after this initial hand you have t800 and C has between t500 and t900.

So the minuscule stack's presence should not significantly alter your normal aggressive strategy with a short stack on the bubble. If D slowly survives with a minuscule stack, force a play if necessary by pushing any two cards when Player B is the big blind because he is the one most likely to fold. (An exception might occur if A were particularly tight, or D had previously folded for one extra big blind on the bubble.)

Now suppose A and B are maniacs, willing to call t1,100 with a wide range and t400 with almost any two. If you hit a dry run of cards in these conditions, do not force a play. This is because you will be called often by hypothesis, and meanwhile, the big blind will be forced to gamble almost immediately. In these tough conditions, the bubble boy will be determined mostly by the fall of the cards, and you will at least know where you stand (in terms of having to gamble) quickly due to the increased action.

Lastly, suppose you are Player C in one of the blinds and player D pushes. If you are the big blind and A and B have folded, you should call with any two since you are being offered 3-to-1 or better and must therefore seize this positive cEV opportunity to eliminate D. If you are the small blind, you should fold weak or marginal hands, and re-shove stronger hands. Meanwhile, if the big blind calls both you and D, then you still place third or better unless D wins the main pot and the big blind wins the sidepot.

Here is a short example of this latter concept:

You (Player C) are in the small blind with Q♦T♦. A folds under-the-gun, D pushes t400 from the button, and B is waiting to act from the big blind.

You should reraise all-in. Your high suited semi-connectors rank to be the best hand, and the pot is laying you 7-to-4 on a call. You cannot fold such a strong hand getting nearly 2-to-1 pot odds and the chance to knock out D, and smooth-calling is too passive. So reraise all-in.

There are also situations that may arise where Player C is correct to flat-call. For example, suppose A folds under-the-gun, and you (as Player C) have K♠J♣ on the button. B is playing aggressively in the small blind, and D is the big blind with t200 remaining after posting.

Then calling is the correct move by process of elimination. Your hand is too strong to fold since D is on the verge of elimination, and king-jack offsuit figures to be the best of the three hands and is certainly a favorite against D's hand alone. Meanwhile, suppose you push. This would, of course, be the normal play you would make as Player C when D has a larger stack and your t1,100 makes you the short-stack at the table looking to make a move. But here, the aggressive B might re-shove a wide distribution of hands (against few of which would you be a significant favorite), in which case D will fold all but a premium hand and you risk complete equity forfeiture with the minuscule-stack D coasting into third.

But now suppose you call. If B folds, then you play a heads-up pot against D with a probable best hand and a pot padded with t100 from the dead small blind. If B merely completes, then you two have an excellent opportunity to eliminate D through implicit collusion. And if B reraises, then even if D folds and you are forced to fold as well, you have still improved your chip lead over D from 11-to-4 to 9-to-2. This makes a smooth-call the superior play in this situation.

In summary, as Player C, the presence of a minuscule stack is not enough to allow you to get blinded out. D could always rebound, and even if you squeak into the money, you will rarely place higher than third. The only difference with D's involvement, besides the necessity of an occasional short-stacked smooth-call, is that when A and/or B are calling with a wide range, you should rarely force a play with a marginal hand so long as you remain comfortably ahead of D in chips.

Player D's Game Plan

If you are Player D, your game plan is essentially outlined in the sub-chapter on "Playing the Minuscule Stack" starting on page 175 in "Part Three: High-Blind Play." There is one notable exception. Suppose a hand like the following arises:

Player C is under-the-gun playing aggressively. You are the button. B is small blind. A, in the big blind, has been playing recklessly.

C raises all-in. In non-bubble conditions, you should call with any two, as explained in the above-referenced section. But if you are dealt a weak hand, you should fold here, declining to take advantage of the pseudo-dead money since the second shortest stack is pushing with a wide range and the huge stack in the big blind is calling recklessly.

In summary, as Player D, you should be looking to open-shove with any solid hand, or otherwise call an all-in due to the vast pseudo-dead money on the table relative to your stack. The exception is if C is the pusher, you have a weak hand, and A or B are calling with a wide range of hands, then you should usually decline the excellent pot odds and hope C is called and eliminated.

High-Blind
Play: Summary

High-blind play is largely a game of chicken. The blinds are high and rising, and you often find yourself with unplayable cards or prior all-in raisers for many hands in a row. Yet it is here where the money is decided, and it will tend to flow toward the most aggressive. Never get blinded out, even if that means you must push in the dark against tight blinds.

While we did consider examples of passive positive equity plays, such as calling all-ins with weak hands when the pot is laying better than 2-to-1, profiting from sit 'n go's is largely a function of your aggression as the blinds rise and the table shrinks. This is why we encountered situations where pushing any two cards is correct, such as when you will be blinded out the subsequent orbit, or you have the opportunity to open-push on the bubble as chip leader and effective stacks of 10BB or fewer.

Remember, all but the most reckless players want desperately to survive. So force them to react to your analytical yet highly aggressive style of play, and the results will speak for themselves.

Part Four

Sit 'n Go Career Play

Sit 'n Go Career Play

Introduction

So far we have discussed the strategy and theory behind one-table tournaments. Now we turn to pertinent issues in sit 'n go career play. These include such questions as:

- How big a bankroll do I need to prevent going broke at a particular buy-in?

- How does the sit 'n go compare to other forms of no-limit poker play?

- What are the most significant aspects of table selection?

We will give a thorough method for manually reading opponents. We will also discuss additional profit-making tools and tricks available for the online player. These include multi-tabling, which most professionals engage in, and the use of legitimate software for analyzing decisions both as you play and after the game.

Once you master basic sit 'n go strategy, your long-term profits are largely dependent on how well you master such broader issues as opponent reading, table selection, and the remainder of the material in this concluding part on sit 'n go career play. Let's get started.

Sit 'n Go's Versus
Other Forms of Poker

Differences
Between Sit 'n Go's
and Multi-Table Tournaments

First, we observe that moneying in a sit 'n go entails about 30 to 75 minutes of time, and has a payout for the top 30 percent or 33.3 percent of the entrants. Moneying in a multi-table tournament, meanwhile, requires about 4 to 8 hours of time, with only 10 to 20 percent of entrants placing in the money. Since sit 'n go's therefore require less time investment and allow you to money with greater frequency, they are lower variance (i.e., have smaller profit-and-loss fluctuations) than multi-table tournaments.

Second, there is more room for personal strategic preference in a multi-table tournament. In the sit 'n go, the enormous jump from 0 to 20 percent of the prize pool at the bubble makes optimal strategy fairly clear: You should play cautious early to ensure survival into the high blinds, then gradually increase to an aggressive game to maximize your chances of finishing first.

But in a multi-table tournament, there is more room for individual variation. Some winning players adapt a sit 'n go-like strategy, simply trying to play tight early and then increase aggression as the blinds increase and players diminish. But many of the top multi-table tournament players also get involved in lots of small pots, willing to take early risks to exploit big-stacked playing opportunities throughout the tournament. These players often rely on the longer structure and generally greater stack-size-to-blind ratio to base their game on outplaying opponents post-flop to a much greater degree than is possible in fast-structure sit 'n go play.

Another difference between sit 'n go's and multi-table tournaments is that sit 'n go's allow you the opportunity to use table selection to increase the expected return on your investments. As we will discuss below, selecting only those tables that offer weak competition will significantly increase your return on investment. And with sit 'n go's this feat of table selection is readily achievable with mental recognition, notes, and/or software. But in a 400-man multi-table tournament, monitoring the quality of your opposition may be difficult, and choosing your specific table is outright impossible. So table selection is one significant advantage that is available in sit 'n go play yet inapplicable to multi-table tournaments. We will outline the specifics of sit 'n go table selection in a later section.

Next, we have made it a theme in our sit 'n go discussion that you should not be content to coast into the money with a short stack, just glad to be walking away with anything. But in a multi-table tournament, if the prize jumps are significant relative to your bankroll, risk aversion may allow for some "coasting." If moving up one or two rungs in the latter ensures your ability to make profitable future investments, you might reasonably decline a marginally positive equity play.

Lastly, in a multi-table tournament, you will be playing the vast majority against a full table. Indeed, it is only if you make it to the final stages that short-handed play will occur. By contrast, in most of your sit 'n go's, much of your active playing will take place 6-handed or fewer. With the sit 'n go, it is only when you bust out early that you will play entirely at a full table. The same certainly cannot be said about the multi-table tournament.

Consider heads-up play, for instance. An average player will reach heads-up in 20 percent of the 10-man sit 'n go's he enters, whereas the same player will reach heads-up well under 1 percent of the time in a 300-player multi-table tournament. So sit 'n go's favor short-handed skills to a much larger extent than do multi-table tournaments. That is one reason so many of the key hands we examine in this book take place in the context of short-handed play.

There are, therefore, certain fundamental differences between sit 'n go and multi-table tournament play. We now turn our attention to differences between sit 'n go and no-limit cash play.

Differences Between Sit 'n Go's and No-Limit Cash Play

In a cash game, chip expectation is *the* important factor in a decision. By contrast, cEV is only one factor in determining the tournament equity that guides all sit 'n go decisions. So tournament play has another level of complexity in that you must consider not only how a play will affect your stack, but how it will affect your chances of cashing.

However, cash play requires much keener post-flop skills. You must be able to analyze the texture of a flop, have a thorough understanding of implied odds, combine pre-flop and post-flop information to estimate an opponent's holdings, and play in tricky deep-stack situations that rarely arise in fast-paced sit 'n go's where high-blind play dominates.

A cautionary note: Do not apply the strategy in this book to deep-stacked no-limit hold 'em cash games or slower-paced multi-table tournaments when the blinds are small relative to the stacks. While many of the same principles apply, the fundamental differences among these three forms of no-limit are vast enough that separate strategic considerations are required when switching among them.

Winner-Take-All One-Tables

The winner-take-all (WTA) is a form of sit 'n go most commonly held as a qualifier for larger events. Sometimes there is a nominal prize awarded for second place, but the winner must be awarded a significant majority of the prize pool. The single most important concept in winner-take-all play is this:

> Chips no longer change value in the winner-take-all.[10] Therefore you should seize expected chip edges just as you would seize any expected equity edge in a standard sit 'n go.

The reason chips no longer change value is because those who do not finish in first place no longer receive money. For example, suppose you are playing a 10-man WSOP one-table qualifier with 10 players contributing $1,000 each. The winner receives a $10,000 WSOP entry and no other finishing position is paid. Assume each player starts out with t2,000 (in chips).

The initial chip is worth:

$$\$0.50 = \frac{\$1,000 \text{ (in cash)}}{\$2,000 \text{ (in chips)}}$$

The winner ends with t20,000 (in chips) and a $10,000 entry, so each chip is still worth 50 cents.

This mathematical equality corresponds with most players' intuition. Even a novice will seek to avoid fourth place

---

[10] Actually, they do change value if you are clearly the best player and the blinds start low and go up slowly enough to allow you to take advantage of that.

elimination in a standard sit 'n go, whereas there is no corresponding spot in a winner-take-all to spark sudden risk aversion.

So the independent chip model and other equity-based considerations are no longer of use. If you believe that a given play offers your highest chip expectation, you need a compelling a reason to decline.

Question: Is it still correct to play cautiously during low-blind play?

Answer: It depends. There is no longer any reason inherent to the game structure for you to start off cautiously. So you should play a strategy that takes advantage of your strengths. If you are most comfortable making big plays before the flop, as conventional sit 'n go strategy has you, then tend to avoid low-blind situations.

But our initial Jim-Bob race example no longer applies. If you were to double up early in half your winner-take-all games and bust out in the remainder, you would now be precisely a break-even player, excluding any rake.

If you are a skilled no-limit cash player, you might therefore play many pots early, taking advantage of your post-flop ability to seize early edges against your less deep-stacked savvy opponents. So you now have much more strategic flexibility.

In the hand examples that follow, we emphasize the differences between winner-take-alls and conventional sit 'n go's

Hand 4-1

Blinds: t200-t400, t25 ante, 4 players, WTA

Your hand: You (t3,800) have A♠2♣ in the big blind.

Action to you: The cutoff (t400) and button (t400) fold. The reckless small blind, who will push any two cards, moves all in for your entire stack.

Question: Call or fold?

    Answer: Call. In a standard sit 'n go this would be an easy fold since the presence of two players already blinded out compel you to avoid gambling for all your chips without an enormous edge. But since your ace-high is certainly ahead of two random cards on average, you should call since you are better than even-money to win the hand, and the pot is laying you slight odds since there is also t700 in blind/ante money on the table.

Now let us reconsider the above hand and generalize it to answer the following questions:

1. How much better would your hand need to be in this situation to merit a call in a standard sit 'n go?

2. How much worse would your hand need to be to make this situation merit a fold in a winner-take-all?

Answers:

1. We have had software compute positive equity hands for calling here in the standard sit 'n go. According to Power Tools, only aces and kings are positive equity here. In this regard, the hand is similar to the opening hand in the "Bubble Play" sub-chapter starting on page 147 in "Part Three: High-Blind Play." See the analysis there for more details.

2. We now ask the software the same question using chips instead of equity. Thus we see that positive cEV calling

hands are: 22+, J2+, t6+, t2s+, 97o+, 95s+, 87o+, 86s+, 76s+. Looked at alternatively, with the t700 already out, the pot is laying you t4,500-to-t3,800, nearly 6-to-5. So you can call with a slightly below average hand. You should fold hands which are weaker than this. So fold hands as weak or worse than: T♣5♦, 9♠6♣, 9♠4♠, 8♠6♣, and 6♣5♣.

Hand 4-2

Blinds: t10-t20, 9 players

Your hand: You (t1,500) have 4♠4♣ under-the-gun.

Question: Fold, call, or raise?

    Answer: It depends. First, note that we did not specify whether this hand occurs in a winner-take-all or a conventional sit 'n go. In either case, neither folding nor calling can be a big error.

    On the one hand, you have a quality speculative hand and the stacks are relatively deep. On the other hand, you are first to act, and the blinds are low with 9 players remaining.

    For most player-table combinations in a conventional sit 'n go, this latter condition (low blinds, 9 players) takes precendence and you should fold. The exceptions would be if the table was very loose-passive and/or your natural strengths were in deep-stacked play.

    But in a winner-take-all, the "low blinds 9 players remaining" clause is irrelevant since the prize pool is awarded entirely to the winner. So for most player-table combinations, calling here confers a positive chip expectation, and so you should call.

    To summarize, if you would normally fold this hand in a cash game, then you should fold in both the sit 'n go and winner-take-all. If you would normally call in a cash game, then you should call in the winner-take-all, but stay cautious and fold when playing a standard sit 'n go.

Hand 4-3

Blinds: t100-t200, t25 ante, 5 players, WTA

Your hand: You (t2,800) are in the cutoff with the 8♠8♣.
Action: The hijack (t350) folds, and you raise to t550. The button (t235) folds, but the hyper-aggressive small blind (t3,200) re-raises all-in. The big blind (t3,000) folds.

Question: Call or fold?

> **Answer:** Call. As above, in a standard sit 'n go, you would fold since the presence of two minuscule stacks during 5-handed play requires you to avoid certain gambles for all your chips unless you are completely pot-committed (e.g., you are getting 9-to-1 with a hand that could well be best), or you have a premium hand.
>
> But in the winner-take-all, more analysis is required. You are only concerned with placing first, and so your only question is: Will this call earn me chips in the long run? Let us answer this latter question.
>
> The pot is t2,800 (the small blind's bet) + t325 (the big blind and antes) + t550 (your bet) which is approximately t3,700. Meanwhile it costs you t2,800 – t550 = t2,250 to call. So you are being offered considerably better than 3-to-2. Meanwhile, against a hyper-aggressive player, you figure to be at least even money on average. This is because most of the time he is pushing two overcards and you are a slight favorite. If he is pushing a pair, about half are above and half are beneath yours. He could also be pushing a hand like A♥5♥, making you better than 2-to1, or a stone bluff making you a 70-to-30 or even an 85-to-15 favorite.

Indeed, asking Pokerstove how well we do on average when the villain is re-stealing the top 15 percent of the starting hands, we learn that we are only an 11-to-9 underdog. So your call is definitely a chip-earner, and therefore you should call in a winner-take-all in this spot.

We conclude this section by addressing the practical questions of where to find these less-common winner-take-alls, and whether you are better off playing those you find or sticking with the standard sit 'n go.

The winner-take-all is found as stated above most commonly as a qualifier for larger events. For example, a poker site has a nightly $100 buy-in no-limit multi-table tournament. Since many smaller stakes players want a chance to compete for a greater prize pool, there is demand for a smaller buy-in satellite. This satellite may take the form of a 10-man $11+$1 1-table, with the winner taking an entry ticket to the $100 multi-table tournament and second getting $10 back. Since the winner receives the vast bulk of the prize pool, this type of satellite is effectively a winner-take-all.

You should not play a winner-take-all if the winner's prize is not worth at least its cash equivalent to you. (For example, if you valued the $100 tournament above at $85 due to stiff competition, an inconvenient time, etc., then it would obviously not be a worthwhile investment.) You should also believe that your advantage in the winner-take-all (i.e., due to your relative skills and opposition) is greater than for a similar buy-in sit 'n go. This is because if your advantage is the same in equal buy-in sit 'n go's and winner-take-alls, then your average profit per tournament will be the same in both, but the variance will be higher in the winner-take-all. Assuming you prefer minimizing risk when all else is equal, you should therefore be more inclined to playing the sit 'n go. This is because the actual profits you realize from a winner-take-all will vary much more relative to your theoretical average profit in comparison to a three-places-paid sit 'n go.

With the above caveats, there may be many very profitable winner-take-all opportunities. For example, suppose you found a large number of winner-take-alls being offered for the World Series of Poker. You will probably earn higher profits playing these than standard $1,000 buy-in sit 'n go's. There will be many more recreational players at the winner-take-all who "want their shot at the big one," and so your opposition will tend to be weaker. Furthermore, if you cannot sell the first seat you earn, you may still sell subsequent seats won for their stated cash value. These favorable conditions may be ample reason for some players to choose the winner-take-all over the conventional sit 'n go when given the choice.

Profit-Increasing Skills and Techniques

Hand Reading Skills

While software is available to provide useful statistics on your opponents (see below), hand reading can potentially provide crucial information quicker and/or more accurately. Also, software may always fail, or you might find yourself playing in a live tournament or cash game where purely brain-powered hand reading skills will be necessary for success.

The key to player-reading mastery is the method of progression. You must start by paying attention to a limited amount of important information and build from this foundation. Not only will you gain solid reading skills through progression, but the basic reads you start with are also the most profitable.

Step No. 1: Basic Reading of One Opponent. Your first assignment is to determine, each time you sit down at a table, whether the opponent to your immediate left is loose, tight, or neither. Do this by assessing how frequently he enters pots and by looking back over the play of the hand in light of cards he reveals at the showdown.

For example, if your opponent is folding almost any hand when he's not a blind, he is probably tight. If he shows down with

after calling an early position pre-flop raise, then he is probably loose. Always make a player note of what you find for future reference.

Notice that both examples require active observation on your part. For pot-entering frequency, while you do not need to calculate exact statistics, you must still make a qualitative assessment that your opponent is entering the pot more often, less often, or about as often as you would expect. Meanwhile, learning from shown cards requires going back over your opponent's earlier actions and looking for loose or tight behavior based on what cards he showed down with. It is therefore critical that you pay attention to what this one opponent is doing.

Making a regular habit of observing your opponents is the primary skill we are trying to develop, and so consistent reading, no matter how limited the scope, is paramount. Never sit down at the table without doing at least this basic step.

If you feel that your left-most opponent is neither particularly tight nor loose, move on. Rather than force a read, choose another opponent and try again. It is better to lack information than to act on false information. Get to the point where every time you play you have one confident tight-loose read.

Step No. 2: Basic Reading of Many Opponents. After you have become comfortable with Step No. 1, slowly begin adding more players. Your leftmost opponent. Your two leftmost opponents. Your two leftmost opponents and the table captain (most active player). Continue with this process until you can figure out whether multiple opponents are tight or loose (or neither), in particular:

1-3. Your three leftmost opponents.
4. The player to your right.
5. The chip leader or table captain

One crucial element of this process is the *Tentative Read*. Suppose the opponent on your right folds his first seven hands. While you cannot make an informed decision based on seven hands worth of information, you should recognize this player is more likely to be tight than loose. Make a player note of "Tight?" which will signify either moderate or potential tightness.

It is important to type in the question mark to distinguish this note from your more confident reads. Such a note may be helpful in marginal situations where any information is useful. But more importantly, it gives you a basis for future observations. If you see an unfamiliar player make a loose or tight move, you are much less likely to observe and make note of this relative to an opponent on whom you already have a tentative read. This is because you already have a guess as to how your read opponent will behave, and so you are more likely to notice when this read is confirmed or violated.

Step No. 3: Enhanced Reading of Few Opponents. After enough practice building up opponents, you will be ready for the next step: a more comprehensive read. To ease the transition, return to concentrating on only a couple of opponents.

Now try to pick up more than just a tight-loose characterization of your opponent's play. In particular, you should observe if he plays a passive or aggressive style. Apart from hands shown down, where you may reconstruct your opponent's play and label it passive or aggressive, you may simply observe how often an opponent is calling rather than folding or raising. Lots of calling indicates passivity; raising and folding, aggression.

"Tight-aggressive," "loose-passive" type labels are your primary goal. These give you an excellent capsule summary of how your opponents play. But also note any other exploitable tendencies you happen to notice from your opponents. For instance, note if a player will automatically raise from the big blind if you merely complete from the small blind, or if he makes a habit of limping at high blinds (the coveted HBL).

Step No. 4: Enhanced Reading of Multiple Opponents. At this final step, you must keep track of the tightness/looseness and passiveness/aggressiveness of all your opponents. This entails an enhanced read of the five opponents listed earlier, and a basic read of the remainder.

At this point you will have solid and profitable knowledge of how your opponents tend to behave. You begin to pick up on exploitable tendencies such as high-blind limping. You avoid marginal blind-steals against loose blinds, sit to the left (where possible) of opponents you have labeled "Loose," and avoid entering pots with the hyper-aggressive tournament chip leader. These skills will play a major role in allowing you to progress to the higher stakes where accurate reading is a necessity.

Showing Hands

When you win a pot before showdown, you have the option of showing or mucking your holecards.

> Never voluntarily show a hand without a strong reason.

By showing, you are offering observant opponents insight into your playing style. Some shows are particularly ill-advised.

Consider, for instance, a situation where the cut-off makes a standard blind-stealing raise, and you re-steal all-in with

Your opponent folds. If you make this move from the button, showing is only a small mistake. You are telling your opponent he was probably right to fold against your re-steal, potentially boosting his confidence, but your next re-steal may be received with more respect than it otherwise would. The net effect is likely minor.

But if you make this re-steal from the big blind, showing becomes an automatic mistake. The implication of this show is, "I had a good hand, so I went over you. But if I held a weaker hand, I would not have been so aggressive." You want opponents to fear aggressing on your blind. Never make a show which is contrary to this goal.

Also, remember if you win by betting and then voluntarily show a good hand post-flop, keener opponents will use this information to gain insight on your pre-flop play. For example, if you voluntarily show a set of deuces after a post-flop pot-winning bet, other players will then know how you played that pair of deuces before the flop as well.

So in summary, you should have a very good reason when voluntarily showing your cards. Teaching your opponents how you play is not one of them.

Multi-Tabling

With Internet gambling comes the possibility of playing more than one tournament at once. Multi-tabling (playing two or more sit 'n go's concurrently) has certain pros and cons over playing a single table:

Pros

1. It is easier to stay disciplined and play tight when you are seeing more hands, and therefore more playable cards.

2. You will tend to make more money if you are a winning player.

3. You will generate bonuses at a quicker rate.

Cons

1. You will tend to lose more money if you are a losing player. (Of course, if you study this book, this should not be an issue.)

2. If you are playing multiple hands at different tables, or you are playing one important hand, having to contend with other tables may detract from your ability to make the highest-equity decision.

3. You have less time per table to think specifically about the best strategy to pursue for each particular table based on your opponents, their styles, and exploitable holes (such as excessive risk aversion or predictable button steal-raises).

4. Table selection becomes difficult or impossible when action at already-started tables forces you to concentrate less on the current table you are choosing.

Successful multi-tabling requires negating these cons. Here is a strategy:

Play and concentrate on only one table until you are confident you are a winning player and feel capable of reading opponents and making quick and confident decisions. Start multi-tabling gradually. Rather than start many tables at once, I recommend staggering them at set intervals.

For instance, if you are playing speeds that last up to 35 minutes, start a new table every 20 minutes. This way, at any given time, you are playing at most two tables — one at high blinds, one at low blinds. Since you will be folding most of your low-blind hands, this will allow you to practice contending with an easier second table during the intensive high-blind period of the first table. For the low-blind table, still pick up basic reads on your opponents so you will be prepared to play the important high-blind portion assuming you are still in.

From this point, you can begin starting two tournaments at once, and then progressing on to 3-tabling, 4-tabling, etc. Each time you add another table, give the experience a trial run at a lower buy-in. More tables has a point of diminishing returns. So never play more tables than you feel comfortable handling.

One more point on multi-tabling. It is possible to not multi-table, yet still multi-task. This is the author's preferred approach. Here is an example. Begin a non-speed sit 'n go, and find a decent turbo sit 'n go to start around the same time. Then play both low-blind sit 'n go's while concurrently doing another activity that would otherwise require its own time investment, such as reading a poker book, doing homework, or even eating. Then concentrate on the mid- high-blind phase of the turbo while handling the low-mid phases of the non-turbo, and finishing by playing the mid-high phase of the non-turbo while finding a new good table to begin at low blinds.

This way you are always multi-tasking, but the most important aspects of your investments — high-blind sit 'n go play — always take first priority.

Software

If you routinely have two or more tables running, or you are investing more than $100 or so each day in sit 'n go's, tracking software becomes a good investment. It consists of a program and interface to gather and display statistics on yourself and your opponents. Each hand, it keeps track of relevant statistics such as which players voluntarily paid to see the flop. This allows you to play more tables / perform more activities, yet still have reads on your opponents.

With one of these commercial programs running, you can see above each opponent's moniker the following statistics (among many other possibilities):

- **VPIP:** Percentage of hands opponent pays chips to see the flop.

- **PFR:** Percentage of hands opponent raises before the flop.

- **AF:** A number quantifying this opponent's aggression after the flop.

- **Hands:** The number of hands the program has observed this opponent to calculate these statistics.

You can also see pot odds displayed at the center of the table, and the odds of your hand improving by the turn and by the river. After using these programs for sufficient time, you will find yourself with a large database of detailed statistics on your own play and results, as well as your opponents. The ways to use this information are considerable. For instance ...

Example No. 1: Take a tough, solid opponent against whom you have played multiple tournaments. Ideally verify that he is indeed a winning player using a commercial database. Examine his stats, both for comparison with your own and to see how he plays when you play against him — avoid such foes when possible.

Then use a freely-available replayer to watch a virtual reenactment of each hand where he made it to showdown so you can watch him play while knowing his cards. (The program will know his cards any time he shows down a winning hand at the river, mucks a losing hand at showdown, or voluntarily shows a hand after all fold.) This not only gives you insight into how to play against this individual, but how you might want to modify your own game after seeing another's strengths.

Example No. 2: Examine your own stats to find leaks in your game. For instance, perhaps you have almost no eighth to tenth finishes, yet an abundance of fifth and sixth place finishes. Then you are probably playing a weak-tight style, failing to switch gears from the correctly cautious low-blind style play to high-blind aggression, and allowing yourself to get blinded out.

There is also a plethora of software that automates calculation-intensive decisions. For example, any time you are unsure whether the Independent Chip Model suggests you should push versus fold, you can input your opponents' stacks and likely calling ranges and receive your expected equity as output. These programs can also make ICM-based recommendations for calling versus folding and re-stealing versus folding.

At the time of the present writing, two popular commercial programs for opponent statistics are *PokerTracker* and *PokerOffice,* and two popular Independent Chip Model programs are *SNG Power Tools* and *SNG Wizard*. However, software is arguably the fastest-changing aspect of online poker, so you should stay aware of what is currently available on the market.

Sit 'n Go
Business Concepts

Buy-in Differences
from $6 to $530 (or More)

Let us ask a simple question. How is it precisely that the opponents in an $11 sit 'n go differ from those in a $530?

Answer: The $530 player wants to gamble for more money than the $11 player. This is all we know with certainty. There are two common reasons why he might have this preference:

1. He has climbed through the lower buy-ins and accumulated a higher bankroll through solid play.

2. He is overconfident, drunk, on tilt, a wealthy recreational gambler, and/or playing a limit above what his bankroll reasonably allows.

Regardless, the differing buy-ins are more similar than many realize. All will feature loose and tight, passive and aggressive, weak and strong players. Nobody wants to get eliminated on the bubble. The higher buy-ins simply have a higher proportion of players who are good at what they are doing.

The most important skill a solid sit 'n go player must have to successfully navigate from low buy-in to high buy-in play is table selection. This is because the higher the buy-in, the more likely unknown players will play well.

Table Selection

Suppose a sit 'n go player is choosing between two seats at different $109 tables. The open seat at Table A features 6 loose-passive players to his right, and 3 weak-tight players to his left. Meanwhile, the seat at Table B features 3 loose-aggressive players to his left, and 6 single-tabling TAGs to his right. Despite his own skill being the same at both tables, the skills and positions of his opponents will have significant affects on his equity.

Let us approximate some numbers. Suppose our Hero is an average player, i.e., his equity at a random table is exactly $100. At both tables, total equity available is a constant $1,000. Consider Table A first. The loose-passive style is a losing one, so suppose each loose-passive player has an equity of $90. Then these six losing players have a combined equity of $540, leaving $460 for the remaining four players. Hero, with such weak competition and the three tight players directly to his left, should earn considerably more than $109 of this $460.

But the tight-aggressive style is a winning one, so suppose each TAG has an equity of $110. (This minimal hypothesized advantage is due to the stiffness of the competition. Against weak players at other tables, these TAGs would have higher equities.) That leaves $340 for the four remaining players, and with his terrible position and aggressive opposition, Hero's equity figures to be considerably less than $109 of this $340.

Table selection is therefore integral in maintaining a high long-term return on investment. Here are three basic rules to observe when choosing a table.

1. **The more loose and passive your overall opposition, the better.** This is because loose-passive players are losing players and their diminished equities leave more available for everyone else, as in the opening example of this section. So the greater the presence of loose-passive players, and the greater the absence of solid players, the higher your equity.

Loose-aggressive and tight-passive opponents are generally okay as well, so long as they are not seated on your immediate left and right, respectively.

2. **Avoid any table with multiple solid/winning players.** Also avoid any seat where a tight-aggressive player will be to your right (where seat selection is possible). This is because the more winning players you face, the lower the total equity available for everyone else. Also, tight-aggressive players on your right are a nuisance, since they are more likely than average to be around near the bubble, and they will be pushing on your blind much more often than their passive counterparts.

3. **Sit with loose players on your right, tight players to your left if you have seat selection.** This is because the tight player needs a better hand to enter the pot after you have already bet or raised. You then have the loose player acting before you, so you have a much better idea before you enter the pot whether it is likely to be contested. This principle is particularly important in high-blind play. Loose players are more willing to gamble when you blind-steal or make aggressive bubble all-ins, so you are more likely to get an unwelcome call.

The importance of table selection is another reason to limit yourself to few tables at once, as table selection at 3 tables and beyond becomes very difficult. You are already busy with other tables and do not have time to closely monitor new tables for opponents and their positions. This is why you will observe many multi-tablers sitting down first at new tables and simply hoping for the best. These are players whose playing frequency affords them great knowledge of their competition, yet they cannot take advantage of it due to playing volume.

Observing table selection guidelines may result in fewer tournaments/hour, but you will have a noticeably higher expectation per tournament. Particularly at the $55's and up, spending a few minutes to ensure your table presents at least average conditions is a key component to a winning strategy.

When to Play (Times of Day)

You should play when the tables look good. The widely-considered prime time is weekday evenings and nights (EST), as well as weekends. It is true that nights and weekends will offer the most players and tables. If you wish to play 3 or more tables at once, this may be your only option, particularly at the higher buy-ins. But realize that other serious players know this, and so there are often primtime periods with two or more winning sit 'n go pros at most new tables that start for the higher buy-ins.

A Tuesday early afternoon table with loose-passive competition is better than a Saturday night table abounding with pros and multi-tabling rocks. Beyond the $33's or so, therefore, you should avoid having set times to play tournaments. Consider sit 'n go's as part of your work, and have other work available (such as studying a poker book or completing coursework). Then you will not be pressured to take an unfavorable seat simply to have something to do.

Sit 'n Go Business Concepts Summarized

A sit 'n go business is similar to any other business enterprise. It starts with initial capital that you supply yourself. For instance, you deposit $250 into an online poker site. Then you repeatedly invest small fractions of this capital, in the form of playing sit 'n go's. So if you have an account balance of $2,500 and play a $55 sit 'n go, this equates to a business investing 2 percent of its $2,500 capitol (plus a fixed commission).

Each investment has a positive expected rate of return (or else you should not be making it), and so probability dictates your business will earn profits. You may either seize these profits for personal use, or reinvest them in the business. For example, if you build from $1,000 to $1,500 playing $22 sit'n go's, you could either cash out the extra $500 as profit and continue playing at the same level, or begin playing for $33 with your higher bankroll. You could also use some of the $500 for a business expense such as computer improvements.

Your should not allow your business to risk going bankrupt, but you don't want to stifle growth either. So what buy-in should you play relative to your bankroll? More specifically, let us ask: How many buy-ins must a winning player at a particular buy-in have before bad luck cannot reasonably cost him his entire bankroll?

The traditional answer is 50 buy-ins, so that you are investing no more than 2 percent of your total bankroll in one particular sit 'n go. For instance, a decent $55 player should have a bankroll of $2,500 minimum.

However, the actual bankroll you should maintain relative to your buy-in of choice is an individual decision. As a sit 'n go hobbyist, you might start with 25 buy-ins. This will allow for a smaller initial investment, and you have the potential to move quickly through weak competition. The downside is you must be willing to risk going broke, as even the strongest player is not immune from a 25 buy-in downstreak or be willing to move to smaller stakes fairly quickly. In this case, you must rebuild from scratch if you choose not to move down and lose your initial bankroll.

On the opposing end of the spectrum, a bankroll of 100 buy-ins leaves you almost entirely immune from natural swings. You will be playing lower stakes games than you normally would, but there is virtually no risk of a terrible downswing busting you out unless of course you don't play that well to begin with.

I would suggest adhering to the 50 buy-in minimum rule, particularly as you get to the $55 level or any level where one buy-in represents a lot of money to you. This is due in part to psychological reasons as it ensures that you cannot lose more than 2 percent of your bankroll in a given tournament. It is also good business advice, and pro sit 'n go play *is* business.

Lastly, the rake is important. For instance, avoid any $6 sit 'n go's due to the double-rake of 20 percent, even if this means you must play $11's sit 'n go's underfunded. Always look for good rake deals, as the rake does add up long-term. For instance, suppose you have an 8 percent return on investment playing rakeless $10 sit 'n go's, and then a rake is introduced so you must pay the house a fee beyond that $10. How does this affect your profits?

Buy-in	Profit after 900 Games (Cash)	Profit After 900 Games (Buy-ins)
$10	$720.00	72
$10.50	$270.00	25.7
$10.80	$0.00	0
$11	-$180.00	-16.4
$12	-$1,080.00	-90

Rather dramatically, so be on the lookout for noticeably above or below-market rake deals.

The Psychology
of Sit 'n Go Play

Decision-Making
Pyschology and its Exploitation

Poker is a game of decisions. You are constantly deciding whether to check, fold, call, bet, or raise, and this choice may be tough. In this section, we provide three general rules to help with the decision-making process.

First, the time you are allotted to make decisions is a limited resource. Most choices will be quick, such as folding

under-the-gun. When more time would help, however, take as much of what you are given as you need. This advice applies even if the decision seems mundane.

For instance, suppose the blinds are t200-t400, and you are the big blind with t1,400 and a weak hand. The cut-off raises all-in for t900, and everyone else folds. This may seem like a small decision, but if you need time to weigh the odds and consequences of a fold versus a call, take the time.

> Never hesitate to spend extra time making a decision, even a "small" one, when you are unsure.

The second two guidelines are related.

Leaving a hand you should play during low-blind play (roughly the first three levels) is rarely a big mistake. However, mistakenly getting involved in a big pot is a clear blunder when the blinds are low. Therefore, if you are unsure during low-blind play, err on the conservative side of making a smaller potential mistake and simply leave the hand. This is particularly true when the pot is small at the time of your decision.

> Tend to check/fold, or otherwise abandon the hand, when you are unsure what to do and the blinds are low.

A contrasting principle applies during high-blind play. If the blinds are high and/or you are short-stacked, then you should continue when in doubt. You cannot allow yourself to get blinded out, and thus you cannot afford to let a good opportunity pass. When in doubt, therefore, continue with the hand. This is particularly true if you are the aggressor with a stack of 3 to 8BB.

> Tend to bet/raise, or otherwise aggressively continue with the hand, when you are unsure what to do and the blinds are high.

Always Think About the Next Move

When playing poker, always think ahead to how your opponent might respond to your move, and what your response, in turn, would be. If you do not know, be less inclined to play the hand that way.

For example, if you raise, what will happen if you are reraised? Suppose you are in the small blind and are considering a steal-raise with a decent hand. If your opponent is passive, then you can probably make an easy fold to a reraise, knowing you are up against a very solid hand. If the big blind is hyper-aggressive and has you covered, however, you will be in a difficult situation. You have a decent hand and (usually) good odds against a player who might reraise many holdings, but do you really want to risk your entire equity in this particular spot? If you do not know the answer to this question, a different play (usually folding or raising all-in yourself) is probably best. So always think ahead to how your present action will affect your future in the hand, and the tournament as a whole.

Hand 4–4

Blinds: t50-t100, 8 players

Your hand: You (t1,100) have 4♠4♣ on the button. The small blind (t1,800) is loose-aggressive. The big blind (t1,400) is tight-aggressive.

Action to you: Everyone folds.

Question: Should you make a standard t300 steal-raise?
   Answer: No. How might your opponents respond to such a raise? If one of the blinds re-raises, a realistic possibility with two aggressive, larger-stacked blinds, you are in a terrible position. You are forced to either be the caller with a low pocket pair frequently ensuring a coin-flip for your tournament life, or surrender over 25 percent of your stack when you are already on the verge of being short-stacked.

   In this particular case, folding is a better play, but simply raising all-in yourself is even better yet. But forethought should convince you that a conventional steal-raise is not the way to go here.

In sit 'n go play, thinking ahead also requires forethought on tournament conditions. In particular, you should be very aware of how much you'll (likely) have after the blinds pass you next, and therefore how urgent it is to make a move.

Hand 4-5

Blinds: t100-t200, 6 players

Your hand: You (t1,500) have K♠8♠ as UTG+1.
Action to you: Everyone folds.

Question: What is your move?

    Answer: Depends on tournament conditions. Suppose the remaining level time is listed as 30 seconds. Then you should push. If you fold, and do not catch cards your next hand, you will be blinded out. The blinds will leave you with a paltry t900, not enough even for a legitimate steal attempt. You desperately need to make a move, and picking up the blinds or even facing a likely gamble with a robust, yet non-premium hand (such as K♠8♠) is better than getting blinded out.[11]

    But now suppose the remaining level time is given as 9 hands. Then you should fold your K♠8♠. You will have over another orbit to make a move, and blind-stealing with t1,200 is fine when the blinds are t100-t200. Furthermore, increasing your chip count from t1,500 to t1,800 is a fine result, but no longer a necessary move to avoid a catastrophic blinding-out.

---

[11] As a side note, if you plan to fold, there are one or two hands before the blinds hit you, and little time remaining before they rise. So make sure to fold instantly since even one or two seconds of delay may mean hundreds in chips worth of lost blind money.

Whether to risk everything in such a marginal situation depends on how urgently you need to make a move, and what the consequences of action/inaction are. This holds for betting and calling. Make the marginal blind-steal if you are in danger of getting blinded out, pass otherwise. Make the all-in call with decent odds if losing leaves you still in contention, but pass if it would cripple you and table conditions are otherwise favorable. And so on.

> Always think ahead as to how your present actions will affect your future tournament status.

Appendix A

What is the Probability of ...?

Included below are the answers to some of the most common hold 'em probability questions.

There are 1,326 distinct hold 'em starting hands. These include 6 of each pocket pair. For example, there are six ways to be dealt pocket aces:

$$A\spadesuit A\clubsuit \quad A\spadesuit A\blacklozenge \quad A\spadesuit A\heartsuit \quad A\clubsuit A\blacklozenge \quad A\clubsuit A\heartsuit \quad A\blacklozenge A\heartsuit$$

There are 16 of each high card hand. For example, there are 16 ace-kings, including 12 offsuit variations, such as A♠K♣ and A♣K♦, and 4 suited variations, such as A♦K♦.

Pair Statistics

What is the probability of ...

- Being dealt a pocket pair? 5.9 percent

$$.059 = \frac{78}{1,326}$$

where 78 is the number of pairs, and

1,326 is the total number of hands

thus your chances of being dealt a pair to start is approximately 1 in 17 or 16-to-1.

- Being dealt a particular pocket pair? 0.45 percent

- Flopping a set (or better)? 11.8 percent

- Making a set (or better) by the river? 19%

Non-Pair Statistics

- Dealt a particular hand (excluding suits)? 1.2%

- Flopping one pair or better (using at least one hole card)? 32.4%

- Flopping two pair (using both hole cards)? 2%

- Two suited cards flopping a flush? 0.8%

- Two suited cards flopping a 4-flush? 10.9%

- How often will at least one ace flop if you are not holding one? 22.6%

$$.226 = 1 - \left(\frac{46}{50}\right)\left(\frac{45}{49}\right)\left(\frac{44}{48}\right)$$

- Same question, by the river? 35.3%

- How often will an ace flop if you are holding one? 17.2%

- Same question, by the river? 27.6%

Appendix B

Pushing Tables

As discussed in the text, there are many factors that determine whether you should push or fold (or make a different play) during high-blind play. The following tables consider stacks of 3BB, 5BB, 7BB, and 10BB from the positions of small blind, button, cutoff, and with multiple players left to act, and asks: what general categories of hands merit a play in these situations? These are only *rough guidelines*, determined by playing experience, the Sklansky-Chubokov numbers,[12] and reasonable assumptions using Pokerstove and the Independent Chip Model (the latter being done by software such as SNG Power Tools and SNG Wizard).

3BB

Pushing Hands with a Stack Size of 3BB

Position	Pushing Hands
Small Blind	Any face card 54s+ 64s + Any two cards 7 or above
Button	Any suited hand with a face card Any two cards 9 or above 64s + 96s +

---

[12] See *No Limit Hold 'em; Theory and Practice* by David Sklansky and Ed Miller.

Cutoff	Any pocket pair, ace, or king Any two cards T or above 54s+ 64s+ 96s+
Against Many Opponents	Any pocket pair Any suited ace or king Any two face cards 54s+

5BB

Pushing Hands with Stack Size of 5BB

Position	Pushing Hands
Small Blind	98o+ 86s+ 54s+ J5o+
Button	all pocket pairs all aces all kings Q4s + Q8o + JTo + J8s +
Cutoff	all pocket pairs all aces all suited kings 54s+ 86s+

	K8o+ Q6s+ Any two cards T or higher
Against Many Opponents	Any pocket pair Any suited ace A8o+ Any two suited cards T or higher AK, AQ, KQ, and KJ 54s+

7BB

Pushing Hands with Stack Size of 7BB	
Position	**Pushing Hands**
Small Blind	Any pocket pair, ace or king Any suited hand with a face card T9o 54s+ 64s+
Button	Any pocket pair Any ace Any suited king QT+ Any two face cards 54s+
Cutoff	54s+ 22+ A6o+ A2s+ K8o+

	K4s+ Any two face cards Any two suited cards T or higher T8s+ QTo
Against Many Opponents	77+ 98s+ A6s+ ATo+ Any two suited cards T or higher KQ

10BB

Pushing Hands with Stack Size of 10BB	
Position	Pushing Hands
Small Blind	All pocket pairs All aces All kings Q4s + Q8o + JTo + J8s +
Button	All pocket pairs All aces KTo + K8s + QTs +
Cutoff	77+ Any two suited face cards

	A8o+ A6s+ KTs
Against Many Opponents	Avoid pushing with 10 or more blinds against more than 3 opponents (even if hand is worth playing, a smaller raise is usually better)

Appendix C

Drawing Odds Chart

It is imperative to know the odds of improving your hand when deciding your action at the flop or turn. So here is a chart with that information which you should keep with you as you play until you can approximate such odds quickly on your own (or via software). Note the oft-observed "rule of 2:"

> The probability of improving at the turn is approximately 2 times the total number of cards that improve your hand
>
> The probability of improving at the flop is approximately 4 times the total number of cards that improve your hand.[13]

Note that if you have an ace on a board of low cards, there are three cards that improve your hand, not one. This is because there are aces of three remaining suits unaccounted for. However, before you decide you are getting the odds you need to call, ensure the presence of three conditions:

1. **Your call closes the action.** If there are other still-active opponents when you are making your decision, realize these players may raise, making you pay a much steeper price or forcing you out of the hand entirely.

---

[13] This approximation produces a significant over estimate for hands with a large number of outs, i.e., more than 10 outs.

2. **If you do improve, you will not have improved to a second-best hand.** For instance, with your ace on a raggedy flop, improving against a player with a made set does not help much. In fact, it may cause you to lose a significant amount of chips. Until you develop keen hand-reading skills, err on the conservative side and discount outs that may only improve you to a loser with a better hand.

3. **Consider raising instead when appropriate.** Suppose your call closes the action, you are drawing to what you believe is the best hand, and you are getting the odds for a call. Sometimes you should raise instead! Recall that a raise gives you the opportunity to win the pot immediately, or build a larger pot when you have a monster. For instance, if you hold 5♦4♦ and the flop comes J♥3♦2♦ with a single opponent who leads out betting, you should strongly consider raising immediately.

We now suppose all factors lead to an odds-based call/fold decision. Then you should know these odds cold. (Note: 1 Card Percentages are average of turn and river, i.e., 46.5 denominator.)

Type of Draw[14]	No. of Outs	Chance of Hitting an Out with One Card to Come (%)	Odds Against Hitting an Out with One Card to Come	Chance of Hitting an Out with Two Cards to Come (%)	Odds Against Hitting an Out with Two Cards to Come
Trips — Quads	1	2.2	45.5	4.3	22.5
Pocket Pair — Set	2	4.3	22.3	8.4	10.9

[14] Please note that in most cases, the draws listed in this table represent only one example of a type of draw resulting in the specified number of outs. For example, a pocket pair with a four flush drawing to a set or flush represents an alternative example of an 11 out draw.

Type of Draw	No. of Outs	Chance of Hitting an Out with One Card to Come (%)	Odds Against Hitting an Out with One Card to Come	Chance of Hitting an Out with Two Cards to Come (%)	Odds Against Hitting an Out with Two Cards to Come
One Overcard — One Overpair	3	6.5	14.5	12.5	7.0
Gutshot Straight Draw — Straight	4	8.6	10.6	16.5	5.1
One Pair — Two Pair or Trips	5	10.8	8.3	20.4	3.9
Two Overcards — An Overpair	6	12.9	6.8	24.1	3.1
Gutshot Draw + One Overcard — Straight or Overpair	7	15.1	5.6	27.8	2.6
Open Ended Straight Draw — Straight	8	17.2	4.8	31.5	2.2
Four Cards to a Flush — Flush	9	19.4	4.2	35.0	1.9
Gutshot Draw + Two Overcards — Straight or Overpair	10	21.5	3.7	38.4	1.6
Open Ended Straight Draw + One Overcard — Straight or Overpair	11	23.7	3.2	41.7	1.4
Flush Draw + Gutshot Draw — Flush or Straight	12	25.8	2.9	45.0	1.2

Type of Draw	No. of Outs	Chance of Hitting an Out with One Card to Come (%)	Odds Against Hitting an Out with One Card to Come	Chance of Hitting an Out with Two Cards to Come (%)	Odds Against Hitting an Out with Two Cards to Come
Open-Ended Straight Draw + Pair — Straight, Two-pair, or Trips	13	28.0	2.6	48.1	1.1
Flush Draw + Pair — Flush, Two-Pair, or Trips	14	30.1	2.3	51.2	1.0
Flush Draw + Open Ended Straight Draw — Flush or Straight	15	32.3	2.1	54.1	0.8

Appendix D

Pre-flop Hand Probabilities

A "bad beat" is often much less bad than it seems as few hand oppositions in pre-flop hold 'em are huge favorites over others. It is difficult to be worse than a 2-to-1 underdog (such that you win 1 out of 3 times). Indeed, being worse than 2-to-1 usually requires you to be up against an overpair to your two low cards. Lastly, note the significant increase in win probabilities when your cards have suited or connected potential as well.

Pre-Flop Match-Up	Examples	Favorite
Two Overcards versus Two Undercards	AK versus 72 AK versus 54s	68-to-32 59-to-41
One Overcard, Two Cards In-Between	A5 versus K8 A5 versus T9	60-to-40 55-to-45
One Overcard, One Card In-Between	A6 versus Q2 A6 versus Q2s	64-to-36 60-to-40
Pair versus Two Overcards	22 versus J5 22 versus T9s	53-to-47 46-to-54
Pair versus One Overcard	66 versus K6 66 versus K5	69-to-31 70-to-30
Pair versus Two Undercards	KK versus Q6 KK versus 54s	88-to-12 77-to-23
Overpair versus Underpair	KK versus 33	81-to-19

Appendix E

Your Hand
Versus a Random Hand

(A random hand means an equal chance of being dealt any of the 1,325 starting hands, taking into account the two already-known cards.)

In light of our discussion on pushing in the dark, we ask the freeware PokerStove how several categories of hands fare against a random hand.

Hand	Wins Against a Random Hand (%)
72o	35-to-65
AA	85-to-15
22	51-to-49
54s	41-to-59
QT	57-to-43
J5	47-to-53
98o	48-to-52

Appendix F

Consecutive Hands Starting as the Bubble Short Stack

We are 60 hands into a PokerStars $114 no-limit hold 'em turbo sit 'n go with 5 minutes blind levels. Four players remain:

1.   Jimmy: Chip leader with about t6,000. Nondescript style with VPIP/PFR/AF of 22/13/1.1 after 60 hands.

(See the section on "Software" for details on these statistics.)

2.   Todd: Second in chips with about t4,000. Tight-aggressive regular with 13/12/2.0 after 620 hands.

3.   Ox: Third in chips with about t2,200. Appears solid with 11/9/0.8 after 94 hands.

4.   Hero: Short stack with about t1,400. Has tight-aggressive image (for those paying attention, as many players fail to do).

We now follow Hero on his course to conquer the infamous bubble. Blinds start at t100-t200 with a t25 ante, and will rise to t200-t400 (t25 ante) in one hand. Note that Hero's cards are often not presented first. This is because other factors are frequently just as important in the decision-making process, and you should make a habit of considering what is important in the hand to come before your cards are even dealt.

Hand No. 1

Players

- Todd is UTG with t3,985.
- Hero is the button with t1,355.
- Jimmy is the small blind with t5,865.
- Ox is the big blind with t1,995.

(We will follow our previous convention of listing the blinds' stacks *after* they have posted their blind.)

Discussion: Hero is on the button with a mere t1,355 left. The blinds will rise to t200-t400 next hand, and the starting pot is t400 with antes. Ox is the big blind with a stack under t2,000 after posting. Therefore conditions are perfect for Hero to push, and unless Todd opens the pot, Hero's cards are irrelevant. (See "How Not to Get Blinded Out" starting on page 135 in "Part Three: High-Blind Play" for more on this topic.)

Action: Todd folds. Hero happily pushes his Q♣7♠. Both blinds fold.

Now the blinds rise to t200-t400 with a t25 ante.

Hand No. 2

Players

- Hero is UTG with t1,970.
- Jimmy is the button with t5,840.
- Ox is the small blind with t1,770.
- Todd is the big blind with t3,560.

Discussion: Hero is under-the-gun with t1,730. The starting pot is t700 and the blinds hit us next hand, so rather than get blinded out, we push any two. So our game plan is to cover the screen with your left hand, and blindly push any two with your right.

Action: We do so, everyone folds, and we observe that we actually had A♥J♣. We gain t700 and are now safe for at least one more orbit.

This hand and the previous hand serve to re-enforce the push-in-the-dark semi-bluff concept discussed previously. When you push blindly, everyone can (and often will) fold, and if you are called, your hand might actually be strong or at least have significant draw-out potential.

Hand No. 3

Players

- Jimmy is UTG with t5,815.
- Ox is the button with t1,745.
- Todd is the small blind with t3,335.
- Hero is the big blind with t2,005.

Discussion: Now we are in the big blind with t2,005 after posting. We look down at 3♦2♣. If everyone folds, great. Otherwise we cannot call off most or all of our chips on the bubble with a trash hand.

Action: Jimmy shoves under-the-gun as he should be doing with a wide range of hands here as chip leader on the bubble. We fold.

Hand No. 4

Players

- Ox is UTG with t1,720.
- Todd is the button with t3,310.
- Hero is the small blind with t1,780.
- Jimmy is the big blind with t6,090.

Discussion: Now we are the small blind with t1,780 after posting. Since Jimmy might call with a wide range, we will need a solid hand to steal his blind.

Action: Ox pushes all-in for t1,720 from under-the-gun. We will need a very strong hand to call this bet. Alas, T♣4♥ does not qualify and we fold.

Hand No. 5

Players

- Todd is UTG with t3,285.
- Hero is the button with t1,755.
- Jimmy is the small blind with t5,865.
- Ox is the big blind with t1,995.

Discussion: The good news: We have passed the blinds. The bad news: With 4BB in chips, we *must* shove one of the next two hands, or we are blinded out.

If Todd folds from UTG we will push any non-trash hand since Ox is a short-stacked big blind who will not want to bubble out. If Todd pushes, then we fold any non-premium hand and push Hand No. 6 in the dark.

Action: We look down to find 7♠7♥. Todd folds. Since a weak/marginal hand such as mid offsuit connectors (e.g., 7♥6♠) would have been sufficient, we happily push our mid pocket pair here. Both blinds fold and we collect t700.

Hand No. 6

Players

- Hero is UTG with t2,430.
- Jimmy is the button with t5,840.
- Ox is the small blind with t1,770.
- Todd is big blind with t2,860.

Discussion: With a stack of 6BB and relatively low antes, we may fold and let the blinds pass us again. However, since Jimmy is not looking to make a call here without a real hand, and our stack is large enough to cripple the blinds, we want to maximize chip accumulation by exploiting bubble passivity. So we will push any decent hand such as: Q♥6♥, 2♣2♠, 9♦8♦, K♣5♥.

Action: The cards are dealt and we find ourselves with J♦7♦. Since this hand is suited and has slight connectedness and moderate high-card value as well, it is indeed good enough to push. Everyone folds, and our semi-bluff has succeeded. We gain another t700, an excellent result putting us in serious position to cripple the table through high-blind aggression.

Hand No. 7

Players

- Jimmy is UTG with t5,815.
- Ox is the button with t1,745.
- Todd is the small blind with t2,635.
- Hero is the big blind with t2,705.

Discussion: We are now second in chips as the big blind. We will need a very strong hand to call if Jimmy or Todd pushes, and a fairly strong hand to call a short-stacked push from Ox as well.

Action: All fold to Todd in the small blind who pushes. Our Q♦8♦, while quite possibly ahead of Todd's holding, is much too weak to gamble with in this spot. We fold.

Hand No. 8

Players

- Ox is UTG with t1,720.
- Todd is the button with t3,310.
- Hero is the small blind with t2,480.
- Jimmy is the big blind with t5,390.

Discussion: We will need a moderately strong hand to shove t2,680 into the chip leader's stack, and a premium hand to call a prior all-in.

Action: Ox and Todd fold, and we look down to find the 8♣8♥. Any ace-high or pocket pair hand is more than sufficient in this spot, and so we again shove our mid pocket pair. Jimmy folds.

Hand No. 9

Players

- Todd is UTG with t3,285.
- Hero is the button with t3,155.
- Jimmy is the small blind with t5,165.
- Ox is the big blind with t1,295.

Discussion: It now appears that Ox is going to be the bubble boy. Since our stack is large enough to damage or eliminate any of our remaining opponents, we would normally be looking to push widely if Todd folds under-the-gun. But there is a problem. Ox is too short-stacked! He only has around 3BB after posting, and so might make a desperation call with a weak hand since he is already being blinded-out. This lowers our fold equity signficantly, and so even if we have the opportunity to open-push, we will need a stronger than normal hand to do so.

Action: We are dealt the 8♣2♥, Todd folds, and we follow suit. Jimmy folds as well, and Ox takes the pot uncontested as big blind.

Hand No. 10

Players

- Hero is UTG with t3,130.
- Jimmy is the button with t5,140.
- Ox is the small blind with t1,770.
- Todd is the big blind with t2,860.

Discussion: In our theme of bubble aggression, we are looking to push fairly wide here, particularly since the blinds will need a real hand to call, and Jimmy has shown some recent reluctance to enter pots.

Action: We are dealt the A♠6♥, and since a low-mid ace is a legitimate hand in 4-way play, it is certainly good enough to push. We raise all-in and everyone folds.

Hand No. 11

Players

- Jimmy is UTG with t5,115.
- Ox is the button with t1,745.
- Todd is the small blind with t2,635.
- Hero is the big blind with t3,405.

Discussion: We are looking pretty good with 8 to 9BB after posting. If Jimmy or Todd push, we will have to fold all but a premium hand (particularly against Jimmy since we would still have a very small stack after a loss against Todd). If Ox pushes, we will have to evaluate.

Action: The cards are dealt and we get the T♠5♥. Jimmy folds. Ox pushes t1,745. Todd folds.

Discussion: Let us analyze whether a call is justified. The pot is t1,745 (Ox's bet) + t700 (blind/ante money) which is t2,450, and it costs us t1,345 to call. We are getting worse than 2-to-1 with a weak ten-high. It is debateable whether this call is even positive cEV, and we are not looking to risk our excellent chip position on a certain gamble that may even be a chip-loser.

Action: We fold and Ox takes the pot.

Hand No. 12

Players

- Ox is UTG with t2,420.
- Todd is the button with t2,610.
- Hero is the small blind with t2,980.
- Jimmy is the big blind with t4,690.

Discussion: The stacks are becoming more even, and Jimmy's passivity is slowly costing him his chip lead. When you are chip leader during high-blind bubble play you must aggress relentlessly. Jimmy has missed several good opportunities, and as second in chips, we are happy to observe some timidity relative to his optimal strategy as bubble chip leader.

If Ox or Todd raise here, we must fold any non-premium hand. Otherwise we will push widely against Jimmy to take another t700.

Action: We are dealt K♠6♠. A mid-suited king is certainly good enough for a blind-steal, but when Todd open-shoves for almost all our chips, we have no choice but to fold. Jimmy folds as well.

Hand No. 13

Players

- Todd is UTG with t3,285.
- Hero is the button with t3,155.
- Jimmy is the small blind with t4,465.
- Ox is the big blind with t1,995.

Discussion: All-in raises, even smaller ones, are simply not getting called at this table. With that in mind, we will push any decent hand from the button if Todd folds.

Action: Todd folds. But when the deck gives us T♣3♥, we fold.

Discussion: A weak ten-high is simply too poor a hand when pushing 7BB into two players, one of whom is the chip leader. That's because we have a trash hand, and it is probably not worth risking bubble elimination with two active players left, one of whom has us covered, while meanwhile we face no compulsion to make an immediate move.

Action: Jimmy takes some initiative here and follows our fold by pushing on Ox's blind. Ox folds.

Hand No. 14

Players

- Hero is UTG with t3,130.
- Jimmy is the button with t5,140.
- Ox is the small blind with t1,770.
- Todd is the big blind with t2,860.

Discussion: The blinds are about to go up to t300-t600, and the table is passive. We will again push widely.

Action: We are dealt 9♥4♦ which is too weak a holding to play. So we fold. Jimmy raises all-in. Perhaps he has finally realized that he can take advantage of being chip leader, or maybe he has just hit some cards. This is something we will have to look out for. In the meanwhile, both blinds fold.

The blinds now rise to t300-t600 with a t50 ante.

Hand No. 15

Players

- Jimmy is UTG with t5,815.
- Ox is the button with t1,745.
- Todd is the small blind with t2,535.
- Hero is the big blind with t2,505.

Discussion: This situation is similar to Hand No. 11. Hopefully everyone folds. If not, we will most likely fold to an all-in.

Action: The cards are dealt and we have K♣8♥. Jimmy folds (a mistake regardless of his holding in this situation), and Ox raises all-in for t1,745. Todd folds. We call.

Discussion: There are several reasons why we elected to call. The starting pot is t1,100 with the blinds/antes, and Ox adds another t1,745 with his bet. So we are being laid t2,345-to-t1,145, or a bit better than 2-to-1.

Next, since Ox is a fairly solid player, he knows he must push widely here as he is already on the verge of being blinded out. On balance, we are probably at least even with Ox's pushing range while getting better than 2-to-1 from the pot. Furthermore, a call and loss still leaves us in some contention, while a fold here leaves us with only 4BB in chips — so we will need to make a move soon anyway. These highly favorable conditions make this spot the time to act even if it requires being the caller.

Action: Ox flips 4♣3♣. An apparently pitiful holding, but the hand does have suitedness and connectedness. Since Ox needed desperately to make a move anyway, and all-ins were not being called, his push here is reasonable.

The board comes: T♦9♠8♠7♥7♠. An excellent result.

Discussion: Our opponents should now see us as blind-defensive by calling a bubble all-in with a king-high hand. More importantly, the extra chips we won will allow us to play with ruthless aggression during the remainder of high-blind play.

Hand No. 16

Players

- Todd is the button with t2,485.
- Hero is the small blind with t4,950.
- Jimmy is the big blind with t5,165.

Discussion: We are now down to 3-handed play with a stack of around t5,000 after posting. Now that we are in the money, both pushing and calling will probably occur more frequently, so we have to really assess how our hands stack up to our opponents' probable holdings, pot odds, etc.

If Todd folds this hand, we should certainly push a wide range of hands against Jimmy, since he will not want Todd to coast into second as he has twice as many chips.

Action: We are dealt the K♠9♠, a hand certainly good enough to push into Jimmy from the small blind. But Todd beats us into the pot with a t2,485 all-in.

Question: Do we fold, call, or raise?

Answer: First, note that calling is out of the question. This is because if Jimmy comes over top, we will be pot-committed to call, and so we may as well make the bet ourselves.

Reraising rather than calling also increases our equity if Jimmy had intended to smooth-call Todd's raise since the t1,050 of pseudo-dead blind/ante money is huge, and we must protect our share of it to maximize our expected chip gain.

And indeed this reraise is precisely the move to make. Assuming Jimmy folds (as he very likely will without a very strong hand when faced with an all-in followed by a reshove), the pot is t2,485 + t1,050 which is approximately t3,600, and it costs around t2,200 to call. A high suited king compares quite favorably to Todd's pushing range, and with the pseudo-dead money bumping our pot odds to better than 3-to-2, this hand should be played.

Action: We reraise all-in. Todd flips over 2♠2♣. The board comes: K♣Q♥J♣6♥4♥. We win the race, and prepare for heads up play.

Lastly, note that if Jimmy held a monster in that situation, we would only bust out third if Todd outdrew him to win the main pot, and we still lost the side pot — an unlikely combination of events indeed.

Hand No. 17

Players

- Hero is the button with t8,085.
- Jimmy is the big blind with t4,515.

Discussion: Since Jimmy is the short stack and we are playing head's up, his stack is our effective stack. (See "Adjusting to Different Stack Sizes" starting on page 123 in "Part Two: Mid-Blind Play" for more on this topic.) Therefore any hand worth playing — namely any hand with some combination of high card, suitedness, or connectedness potential — should be pushed all-in. Indeed, blindly pushing any two cards would be a reasonable strategy here.

Action: We are dealt Q♠3♠. This suited queen easily qualifies and so we push. Jimmy calls, showing A♠J♣.

Discussion: Our push was still correct despite Jimmy having picked up a monster for heads up play. Also, even though we are behind, our suited queen leaves us a full 40 percent to draw out.

Action: The board comes: K♥4♥4♦3♦2♠ and we indeed make a minor drawout and take down the tournament.

This combination of high-blind aggression and analysis of important tournament factors (along with a little luck, of course) led us from the bubble short stack to sit 'n go victor. If there is one lesson to take away from these hands, it is that you must do whatever it takes to maximize late-stage chip accumulation, and you should not let your cards prevent you from exploiting an otherwise favorable situation. Also, I want to mention that *The Mathematics of Poker* by Bill Chen and Jerrod Ankenman cover optimum heads-up push strategy for those who want to read more in this area.

Index

GETTING STARTED IN HOLD 'EM
Ed Miller
$17.95

No Limit Hold 'em
Overview
Understanding Stack Size

Limit Hold 'em
Sample Hands
Preflop Standards

TOURN
Satellite S

INSIDE THE POKER MIND
Essays on Hold 'em
and General Poker Concepts
by JOHN FEENEY, Ph.D.
US $24.95

TOPICS INCLUDE:
• Playing Too Many Hands
• Self-Weighting
• Short-Hand
• The Stra
• Counter
• A Pok
• Tho
the

DAVID
Stra

Small Stakes Hold 'em
Ed MILLER   David SKLANSKY   Mason MALMUTH
US $24.9
Winning Big With Expert Play

The definitive guid
loose games and ama

THE PSYCHOLOGY OF POKER
by
Alan N. Schoonmaker, Ph.D.
US $24.95

Includes:

THE RIGHT STUFF
THE RIGHT SKILLS
STYLES AND RATINGS
THE LOOSE-AGGRESSIVE PLAYER
THE LOOSE-PASSIVE PLAYER
THE TIGHT-PASSIVE PLAYER
THE TIGHT-AGGRESSIVE PLAYER
OUR DEADLY SINS

DAVID SKLANSKY
Strategy Consultant

PROFESSIONAL NO-LIMIT HOLD 'EM
US $29.95

VOLUME ONE

FLYNN   SUNNY MEHTA   ED M

Winning In Tough Hold 'em Games
US $29.95
Short-Handed and
High-Stakes Concepts and
Theory for Limit Hold 'em

• Pre-Flop Play
• Blind Defense
• Playing Heads-Up Post-Flop
• Semi-Bluffing
• Miscellaneous Topics
• Hands With Stox
• Quizzes

Nick "Stoxtrader" Grudzien
Geoff "Zobags" Herzog

Sit 'n Go Strategy
EXPERT ADVICE FOR BEATING
ONE-TABLE POKER TOURNAMENTS
US $24.95

LOW BLIND PLAY
MID BLIND PLAY
HIGH BLIND PLAY
CAREER PLAY

Collin Moshman

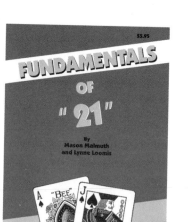